P9-DHL-323

*For Austin, Garrett, Luke, and Stephen*

# FIELDS OF GRACE

This Large Print Book carries the
Seal of Approval of N.A.V.H.

# FIELDS OF GRACE

## FAITH, FRIENDSHIP, AND THE DAY I NEARLY LOST EVERYTHING

## HANNAH LUCE
## WITH ROBIN GABY FISHER

**WHEELER PUBLISHING**
*A part of Gale, Cengage Learning*

GALE
CENGAGE Learning®

Detroit • New York • San Francisco • New Haven, Conn • Waterville, Maine • London

GALE
CENGAGE Learning®

Copyright © 2013 The Hope Project.
Wheeler Publishing, a part of Gale, Cengage Learning.

**ALL RIGHTS RESERVED**
Wheeler Publishing Large Print Hardcover.
The text of this Large Print edition is unabridged.
Other aspects of the book may vary from the original edition.
Set in 16 pt. Plantin.

**LIBRARY OF CONGRESS CATALOGING-IN-PUBLICATION DATA**

Luce, Hannah.
   Fields of grace : faith, friendship, and the day I nearly lost everything / by
Hannah Luce with Robin Gaby Fisher. — Large Print edition.
   pages cm (Wheeler large print hardcover)
   ISBN-13: 978-1-4104-6590-0 (hardcover)
   ISBN-10: 1-4104-6590-X (hardcover)
   1. Luce, Hannah. 2. Christian biography—United States. 3. Airplane crash
survival—Kansas. 4. Large type books. I. Title.
   BR1725.L69A3 2014
   269'.2092—dc23
   [B]                                                                2013041128

Published in 2014 by arrangement with Atria Books, a division of Simon
& Schuster, Inc.

Printed in the United States of America
1 2 3 4 5 6 7 18 17 16 15 14

# CONTENTS

# FOREWORD

This is my story. Of growing up as the daughter of one of the most influential evangelical leaders of our time; of losing my early religious convictions somewhere along the way; and, from that doomed plane ride, of finally finding my faith — the faith two profoundly beautiful souls had insisted was in me all along.

— Hannah Luce

# 1
## ROAD TO REDEMPTION

The closer one gets to realizing his Personal Legend, the more that Personal Legend becomes his true reason for being.
— PAULO COELHO, *THE ALCHEMIST*

The late November sun sinks low on the horizon as I make my way toward the mown cornfield in southwest Kansas, back to the worst day of my life. My backpack is stuffed with a warm blanket, a lavender-scented candle, and a book of matches. I plan to stay awhile, once I get where I'm going. I am still recovering from my injuries, so my movements are slow and shaky, but I am in no rush to beat the dark. This is something I must do.

The first time I was in this rural corner of Middle America was six months ago, in mid-May. It was planting season, and the terrain was lush with burgeoning crops. I remember the spinning fields of green as our plane plunged, sadistically slowly, but stubbornly and ferociously, toward the earth below. Anything I had hoped to see was lost in those spinning fields. I couldn't make out a house or a barn, nor a river or a lake. Not a tractor, or a car, or even a road that looked traveled enough to lead somewhere else. I know all of this because, as the plane was dropping out of the sky, I was already planning my survival, even though I was prepared to die. As hard as I try to forget, I remember every detail from that hellish day. The first signs that our plane was in trouble. The desperate efforts by the boys to try to save us. The resignation I saw in their eyes when the outcome became obvious. (Was it resignation? Or faith?) Searching the faces of my dear friends as we hurtled toward a certain, terrible death. Last words. *Lord have mercy. Christ have mercy. In the name of the Father, the Son, and the Holy Spirit.*

The cornfield is in the middle of nowhere, off a gravel lane that you'd never know was there unless you lived in these parts, or happened upon it for some reason, as I did. I've come here, I think, looking for forgiveness for surviving the crash when everyone else died. I know that I must have mercy on myself before I can begin to seek the kind of purposeful life that my friends deserved. So far, all I have felt is the torrid guilt of being alive when my friends are dead, and the acid torment of my thoughts.

Sometimes, when I'm in the shower, I claw at my scars, hoping to erase my memories of that tragic day. But I will never forget. My scars are a constant reminder. I haven't slept through the night since the crash. Every time I close my eyes I wake up screaming just before the plane slams into the earth. That's when the real torture begins, as I thrash around in my bed with all of the lights in my room turned to bright, afraid to close my eyes again, resisting ghastly flashbacks as I try to make sense of something that will never make any sense.

Five people were aboard that plane, all of us friends from Oral Roberts University, everyone giddy about traveling to a Christian youth conference hosted by my father, the leader of one of the largest evangelical Christian youth ministries in the world. Two of those people, Austin Anderson and Garrett Coble, were my closest friends, and I deeply cared for Garrett, although I never got to tell him so.

I met Austin first, shortly after the start of the fall semester at ORU in 2009. He had recently returned from his second tour of duty in Iraq, and he was studying business. We started talking one day, and soon we were stealing away to a spot beneath the Forty-first Street Bridge in Tulsa where we'd sit by the river, puffing cigars and planning our futures. Austin was a poster boy for the Marines. He was tall and fit, with a blond crew cut and the rough edges of a country boy. He told me stories from the war, and the conflicts he felt about fighting it, and I helped him to explore the struggles with faith that so often result from witnessing the profane effects of combat. He said he liked me because I didn't fit the typical stereotype of the ORU girl, whom he described as someone who drove Daddy's yellow Mustang and majored in finding a husband. I aspired *not* to be that girl, much to the chagrin of my fundamentalist Christian parents. I was a bit of a rebel, a "free thinker" trapped in what I saw as a culture of closed minds. When I wasn't studying church history in the college library, I took long walks alone in the avant-garde neighborhoods of Tulsa, stopping in old bookshops to browse for rare books on things like herbs and witches, or ducking into hookah bars to sit at communal tables and share water pipes of *shisha* with strangers.

"You're such a hippy, Hannah," Austin would say in his country boy twang, shaking his head and laughing. "You and your artsy ways." Austin was a heartthrob. He walked around campus like he was the "It" boy, and he seemed to always have an entourage of cheerleaders on his heels. All of the girls wanted to claim him, but ours was a strictly platonic relationship, and we both liked it that way. He was always trying to fix me up with his friend, Garrett, who was a little bit older and a popular adjunct on campus. "C'mon, Hannah!" Austin would say, elbowing me in a playful way. "He's a good guy, and he really wants to meet you!"

Garrett taught marketing at ORU while he was studying for his Ph.D. in business administration at Oklahoma State University. I'd heard his name because he was popular with the students, but we had never met. Finally, one day, he tagged along with Austin for lunch at our favorite rib place. I thought he was fascinating, if a bit fussy and impatient. Garrett was seven years older than me, and he'd been on Christian mission trips around the world, often with my dad's ministry, as I had, although we'd never crossed paths during that time. We shared a love for travel and an unquenchable thirst for knowledge, but our compatibility pretty much ended there. I'll never forget the first time I looked in his closet. He had the exact same golf shirt in every color. He was clean-cut and conservative. I loved red lipstick and Bob Dylan. I think, for his part, Garrett was drawn to me, at least initially, because of who my father was: the rock star of charismatic Christian teen ministries. As it turned out, he'd attended my father's Christian boot camp with his church group more than a dozen times when he was in his teens, and he said it changed the course of his life. I used to tease him that he had a man crush on Papa.

Our relationship took twists and turns between friendship and romance that first year; we were so drawn to one another, it couldn't be helped. He was the first to initiate any real closeness between us, always inviting me for walks through the park on Riverside, near the university, or hot-tubbing at his house nearby. He had a kind of dorky charm that I was attracted to, which I couldn't even admit to myself. We often cuddled and nuzzled and kissed. Stuff like that. But we were in different places in our lives. He was ready to settle down and have a family. I was a free spirit on the verge of many adventures I had planned for my future.

Garrett and Austin were country boys at heart. They both grew up in small Oklahoma towns, in families with strong Christian values. While I did just about anything to distance myself from what I saw as my oppressive religious background, they were looking for ways to put their faith to work. In fact, that was the purpose of our flight to Council Bluffs, Iowa, on that fateful day in May. They were working with my father's ministry, pitching in to help save a generation of young Christians. I was going to get closer to my dad, to try to atone for the disappointment he felt in me for straying from my faith. I was rudderless and searching for my spirituality, and they couldn't wait to get out there and do their part to change the world. I'll always cherish the photos from our last day together, taken moments before the plane took off. I wanted to document the beginning of our big adventure. There we are, crunched together in the back of the Cessna, the boys in their golf shirts and khakis, me in my big, red sunglasses. I held out my camera and pursed my lips like a supermodel. *C'mon, boys! Smile!* I didn't need to tell them. They woke up smiling.

Austin and Garrett had so much promise and so many grand intentions. So why were they taken so young, before they had a chance to realize their dreams? Why did I live and they die? I have asked myself those very questions relentlessly over the last few months. When the answers don't come, and I'm fraught with angst, I sometimes seek comfort in the airplane-sized bottles of rum and gin that I keep close, but no one knows that, certainly not my parents. Even when I do take something to try to numb my thoughts, the respite from feelings of guilt and remorse are fleeting. I have felt hopelessly alone in my grief. When I've been at my wits' end, I've tried turning to my mother and Papa for, what? Absolution for surviving? Salvation from my dark thoughts? Every time I do, they look at me with expressions of helplessness — and, sometimes, I think, exasperation — then tell me to "give it to Jesus." If only it were that easy.

The field where we crashed is vast, with random clumps of oak and ash trees. I'm not sure of the exact spot where the plane hit, and there's a lot of space to cover, but I have asked to take this trip alone because it is too awfully personal to share. Making my way through shorn stalks of corn, I am guided only by my instincts and the light of

18

the rising, full moon. I am a diminutive girl — five feet two inches, and a hundred pounds last I checked — a mere speck in the wide-open landscape that is rolled out before me, yet rather than feeling lost or overwhelmed, I feel strangely content, the way I do when I wrap myself in the ratty black sweater I keep in my bottom dresser drawer back home, for those chilly nights when nothing else can warm me. This is the place that changed my life and challenged who I was — a rebellious and rather cynical girl who questioned everything about her staunch Christian upbringing, even the existence of God. I'm not that person anymore, I'm sure of it, but I don't know who the postcrash Hannah is. My hope is that I might find some answers in this lonely stretch of rural cropland. Only then can I begin to live again.

The walk through the field is longer than I remember. Except for the crunch of my steps on the leftover corn stalks from the fall harvest, it is as quiet as death. Against my will, my memory fills the silence with the frenzied drone of an airplane in trouble, and I'm transported back to that day and falling from the sky. I freeze in my tracks, but something — what is it? a hand on my back? — pushes me gently forward. Tentative but determined, I press on. A few minutes pass, and I know I am close to the crash site because the energy around me has come alive. My skin prickles with anticipation. It reminds me of the tingly feeling you get when you're at the airport, awaiting the arrival of a boy you really like. You know his flight has landed and he's there, somewhere, in the terminal. You just don't see him. I walk a few steps farther, wondering what will come next, how far I still have to go. That's when I see it, what looks like a pool of shimmering stars. I pull the pocket flashlight from my backpack and shine it on the spot. My heart skips and jumps. A few feet in front of me, scattered around a towering red oak, is what has to be a million bits of metal, reflecting the light from the full moon. That's all that's left of our plane, these tiny pieces of shiny metal. I pick up a handful and tuck them into my bag for safekeeping. They feel like treasure, the last vestiges of my precious friendships.

The oak tree looms over me like a pair of protective arms. Its trunk is scorched and its limbs are twisted and bowed. This is where the plane stopped after it slammed into the ground and careened wildly out of control. I remember seeing it when I was draped over Garrett's lifeless body, half in the plane, half out, trying to free myself from the burning cabin. At first I am stunned, but then lyrics my sister, Charity, wrote for me, in an attempt to lift my sagging spirits, spring to mind. I begin to sing.

Freedom, come recite your joyful strains
Over a thirsty audience
And let her melody whisk us away
To a place we have not wholly known,
To the place we have deemed our own
And while the boughs of the trees are
    weighed down
I'm going to dance
Oh, I will dance
Let her come and play
A song of rest over a restless heart
And in the stillness of her song
A weary mind is beguiled
And we'll walk on holy ground,
Clothed in celestial sound
And when sorrow falls
I'm going to cry tears of joy
I will laugh
Oh, I will laugh.

A chorus of coyotes' howls drowns out my puny voice. The pack can't be more than a few feet away, but it's too dark for me to see. Their howling turns to what sounds like raucous laughter. I grew up in the flatlands of rural eastern Texas, and I know that means they're trying to intimidate me, the trespasser, force me to leave their haunt, but I am undaunted. I belong here, too. This is where I need to be.

I spread my blanket at the foot of the tree and pull the candle and matches from my backpack. As I strike a match to light the wick, I feel the presence of Garrett and Austin bearing into me. It's as if they were just waiting for me to settle in. Yes, it is a physical presence, not some wanton wish, and, in spite of my doubting nature, I know it to be them. My beloved friends are as here with me as they were when we huddled under the bridge, passing a cigar and sharing a beer. I can't help but smile. "I hoped you'd be here," I say. "I knew you would be. You've always been there when I needed you and I've never needed you more than I do now."

A few short months ago, had either of them suggested that they could reach back to me from an afterlife, I would have laughed out loud and unleashed a string of expletives. At which point Garrett, in all of his Christian righteousness, would have cringed with feigned horror, and Austin, Mr. Macho Marine, would have wagged his

22

finger and admonished me in his most stern Oklahoma country boy twang: "Hannah! You swear like a soldier! You need to learn the manners of a lady."

*God, how I've missed you both.*

A gust of wind blows up, and the flame of my candle flickers out. The darkness is absolute, and I listen for the coyotes, but all is quiet now. "I feel you," I say. "I know you're here. There's so much I have to say."

The air is noticeably colder, and I fold the blanket over my legs. "Austin, I'm sorry I couldn't save you. Thank you for taking care of me. I wish I could have taken your place on that plane, and I hate constantly reliving your suffering. I feel so weak. If only I had your courage, your purpose. I get so angry when people tell me I was saved for a reason. What reason? Why did I have the audacity to survive? Why me instead of you? You had more faith than I did.

"Garrett, I wish I'd loved you better. Thank you for loving me. I don't have your strength or your fierce determination. You were a rock for me. What am I supposed to do now that you're not here? I don't even know how to live without suffering anymore. Part of me doesn't want to stop suffering because I'm afraid if I do, a piece of you will be gone. The other part of me can't live

23

with this kind of pain much longer.

"Please, boys, please tell me you forgive me."

Their answers don't come in the way of physical voices, but I can still hear them. It's as if their thoughts are being placed in my head.

*We're happy, Hannah. Really happy. We're where we want to be. We know we encouraged you, supported you, enriched your life. But some things you need to discover on your own. You need to be able to figure things out for yourself. You can mourn, and we love that you do, but you can't mourn forever. You have to dance.*

I think about the lyrics of my sister's song.

And while the boughs of the trees are
    weighed down
I'm going to dance
Oh, I will dance.

*I'll try,* I say. *For you. And for me.*

# 2
## GROWING UP EVANGELICAL

It is the great business of every Christian to save souls. People complain that they do not know how to take hold of this matter. Why, the reason is plain enough; they have never studied it.

— CHARLES GRANDISON FINNEY,
NINETEENTH-CENTURY CHRISTIAN
EVANGELIST,
*LECTURES ON REVIVALS OF RELIGION*

When I was younger, every morning as I went off to school, my father would pat me on the head and say, "Hannah, now go get someone saved today." Not "Get an A!" or "Do you have your homework?" What did any of that matter if we were all going to Hell? And that's where we were headed if we didn't follow God's orders and, first and foremost, spread the Gospel. The first thing Papa did when I got home from school was ask how many more of my classmates were "on fire for Jesus" because of the witnessing I had done. Sometimes I lied. "Five or six," I'd say, when the real answer was none. None, because I wasn't very popular. In fact, I was socially awkward, and drumming up conversations about Jesus wasn't the best way to make friends, not even in Bible-soaked northeast Texas.

I only started attending school when I was thirteen years old, and I didn't fit in, not even with the Christian kids, not in the beginning. I didn't know how to dress or how to be. Before that, I was home-schooled by my mom, and most of my associations were through Papa's ministry. To say I was sheltered would be a gross understatement. My primary education was spent traveling the country with my parents in a converted school bus as they built their fledgling ministry. Once we settled down, they kept me at home for as long as they could to protect me from the wicked ways of the world. Papa said that even in our cloistered evangelical community we had real Christians and fake Christians, and it was up to me to learn how to distinguish between the two. The world looked like a pretty scary place from inside my straitlaced evangelical home. Everyone out there was fighting and fornicating and indulging in every other capital sin under the sun. The only safe place was within my own righteous circle. But when I was old enough for high school, my parents agreed that they had built a strong enough foundation that I could be trusted to ward off the evil influences I was certain to encounter even in a Christian school environment. It was time for me to have the experience of a formal education, and I was both terrified and thrilled at the prospect.

My first year of high school was at the Grace Community Christian School, whose stated mission is "to assist Christian parents in educating, equipping, and encouraging their children to influence the world for Christ." Grace Community was the largest school of its kind in Tyler, Texas, the closest city to my rural hometown of Garden valley, and it was fertile ground for Papa's youth ministry, which he encouraged me to promote to my classmates. I was already an outcast, having started so late, and being a bit of a nerd I didn't earn any additional popularity points when, soon after I got there, I turned over the school directory to Papa, who, in turn, instructed one of his staff to call everyone in it to try to enlist them for one of his missions. Pretty much the whole school knew I was Ron Luce's kid, so they suspected I was behind the conscription campaign. A few of my classmates were bold enough to ask me if I was. *Did you give some mission rep my number? They won't stop calling our house! Thanks a lot!* I'd look down at my feet, gulp, and grit my teeth, knowing I was busted. Still, the next semester I did the same thing all over again. Because it was for God.

Everything was.

Papa was fifteen when he ran away from his mother's home to live with his father and found his way to drugs and alcohol for a spell before a friend took him to church one Sunday, where the preacher's words really resonated with him. Three weeks later, he committed his life to Jesus, and, ironically, when he returned home to his father's house, all of his belongings were piled up on the front porch like a great big "No Trespassing" warning. His stepmother had given his father an ultimatum — Papa or her — and it apparently hadn't been much of an argument. Papa was a teenager and officially homeless. He says he drove away from the house heartbroken, rejected, and talking to God. But as lost as he felt at that moment, he somehow knew he was headed in the right direction. Sure enough, when his pastor found out what had happened, he invited Papa to come and live with him. Papa said that for the first time in his life, he saw what a real family looked like, and he knew that's what he wanted for himself one day.

My parents met while both were attending Oral Roberts University, the Christian college in Tulsa that was founded by the famous charismatic evangelist, the college I would attend after high school, where every class still begins with a prayer. Mom was an art major and Papa was double-majoring in psychology and theology and a year ahead of her. They married in 1984, after Mom got her degree, in a big, formal ceremony with 150 guests in Mom's hometown of Denver. After that, my parents set out to live what they both agreed would be an unconventional life. They had little money and no real plans for the future, but they were both committed to doing something meaningful, something that would help make the world a godlier place.

After living and working in Tulsa for a year, they embarked on a seven-month mission trip to twenty-five Third World countries and discovered what would become their life's work. Papa said they were in Indonesia, in the middle of the largest Muslim nation in the world, when the Lord spoke to their hearts about ministering to the young generation of Americans who needed to know Jesus.

In the summer of 1986, with no regular income and no real idea about how to recruit a following, my parents established Teen Mania Ministries out of a tiny, spare bedroom in their Tulsa apartment. Today, teen ministries are a dime a dozen, and most are struggling for membership because so many young people are abandoning their Christian faith. But back then just about no one was ministering to teens. Papa was a trailblazer in the Christian youth movement. He and my mom traveled all over the country recruiting teens for Christ.

It took some time for the ministry to really get off the ground. Because my parents hadn't yet established themselves, many of the pastors they solicited for support turned them away at first, others canceled appointments, or forgot they had made appointments until the knock at the door. Mom and Papa were living on a wing and a prayer and, on many a night, didn't even know where they would be sleeping. When they were in luck, they'd be put in a Christian host home, but those kinds of accommodations were sporadic and unpredictable. Papa remembers one time, sharing someone's basement with a couple of Great Danes and their litter of yipping puppies. Once, he and Mom drove from Tulsa to upstate New York, where a blizzard had shut down roads and pretty much everything else. When they finally reached the town where they were supposed to speak, Papa found a phone booth and called the youth pastor to announce their arrival. The pastor said he was sorry, but the event had been canceled. No one offered a host home, and my parents didn't have enough money to get a hotel room. They sat all night in their frigid car in the middle of a blinding snowstorm, and they held each other and cried.

I like to think of my parents back then as a couple of idealistic Bohemian lovers on a mission of goodness. Papa gets a kick out of the description, but he says it wasn't quite so romantic. The rejection was dispiriting, and there were many occasions when they weren't offered a church meal and could barely scrape together enough money to eat. Even when they managed to get an audience at a church or a congregant's home, they weren't always asked back. Papa said, back then, he was far from the magnetic speaker he is today. His nerves would get the best of him, and he'd stammer and stutter and sweat so that his whole shirt would be soaked through. He was apparently loud, too. Mom told me they'd go from living room to living room, trying to recruit followers, and Papa preached as if a thousand people were listening, not the ten or twelve who were there.

I was born in 1989, and Papa had gotten a lot better by then. By the time I was five, my sister, Charity, and brother, Cameron, had been born, and the ministry had grown so much that my parents were looking for a permanent place to settle down. As it turned out, the place in Garden valley, Texas, found us. My parents were friends with someone named Melody Green, who, with her husband, Keith Green, founded the well-known Last Days Ministry in Garden valley. Melody contacted them to say she was planning to move away and she'd heard they were looking for a place for their ministry. Keith Green had died in a plane crash several years earlier, along with two of their children and a family of eight who had been visiting from California. (Coincidentally, in 1991, when I was two years old, Papa crashed the small plane he was flying to one of his Christian rallies. He and the two Teen Mania employees who were with him were injured but all of them recovered. It was only a fluke that I wasn't on the plane that day, but twenty-one years later, I wouldn't be so fortunate.)

Anyway, it was an unimaginable tragedy for the Greens, and no one expected Melody to keep the ministry going. She had, though, for more than a decade. But then, during a prayer session, God told her that her work in Texas was done and it was time to take her two remaining children back to her California roots and turn her Garden valley home and nearby four-hundred-acre church property over to someone who would continue to use it for ministering. My parents had outgrown their space in Tulsa, and the Greens' church campus was everything they needed to take Teen Mania to the next step. It had office space as well as classrooms and dorms, which would allow them to hold summer camp and internship programs. And Melody's house was just down the road, close enough to walk to. Papa and Mom couldn't come close to paying what the property was worth, but they told Melody they would pray over it, which they did, day and night. Their answer came when Melody called again to say that the asking price had been reduced to whatever my parents thought they could afford to pay. It wasn't long after that that we packed up our belongings and drove five hours from

Tulsa to northeast Texas to settle into the rural community of Garden valley, as well known for its thriving Christian culture as for its lucrative rose crop.

I was turning six when we moved. We didn't know it yet, but Teen Mania was on the cusp of becoming a mega force in the evangelical Christian world. Papa was consumed with the ministry. He was in a different city every weekend soliciting people for God. *"The devil hates us, and we gotta be ready to fight and not be these passive little lukewarm, namby-pamby, kum-ba-yah, thumb-sucking babies that call themselves Christians!"* While he was on the road, Mom led prayer groups and Bible classes on the Texas campus. My siblings and I were expected to do our part, and although we were all of tender age, we had our work cut out for us. Our parents taught that everything we did was in service to God. We were His warriors, and His wish was our command. Everything was a test, Papa said. If we chose to do what we wanted, rather than what God wanted us to do, we would be living in sin. At that point, even if God still wanted to get through to us, we, as sinners, wouldn't be able to hear his voice. "If you aren't constantly opening yourself up to hear what God has to say then you'll miss people that need to be witnessed to or saved," Papa said.

I'm not saying that we didn't have the kinds of family moments that others do, because we did. Papa loved being with us kids and there were many times when he'd come home from work and we'd do fun things together, whether it was singing or reading or building a tree house out back. But witnessing was our priority. It took precedence over everything else, household chores, studies, music lessons, and the needs of family and friends. As warriors of Christ, we had to spread His word to try to get unchurched people saved from the hell-fire and wrath they had coming in the afterlife, and, in doing so, we would convert even more warriors for the fight. Eventually the entire world would have heard about salvation, and the Rapture would happen. If we, as the messengers of God, didn't do our best before then, the nonbelievers we didn't reach would be doomed to eternal suffering, and we would be denied some of the rewards of Heaven. That was a heavy burden to lay on a kid, but Papa said it, so I believed it to be true.

I took my job seriously. I woke up every morning at 5:00 a.m. to read Bible verses, and I memorized the Roman Road, a series

of verses from the Book of Romans showing the way to salvation. Meanwhile, Papa
was fast becoming a Christian teen's Michael Jackson. He was packing arenas from
Pontiac, Michigan, to Denver, Sacramento,
Houston, and Baton Rouge. Some of his
followers were already disciples of Jesus.
Others were lost and searching. When he
stepped onstage, the audience went wild.
He always gave them a show they'd never
forget. He'd pace from one side of the stage
to the other, with his dog-eared Bible
clutched in his hand, getting the audience
"on fire for Jesus." *When you really fall in
love with Jesus, you fall out of love with the
world! I am praying that you fall so head over
heels, freak of nature in love with the Son of
God that you don't care what ANYBODY else
thinks! JESUS! Use us to dream your dreams.
Use us to show a very dark world how GREAT
YOU ARE!* All over the stadium, young
people would be shedding tears, or falling
on their knees, giving glory to Papa and to
God. It was pretty heady stuff to see your
father as the subject of that kind of hero
worship.

My first "save" was during one of those
events. While Papa was onstage, I went into
one of the public bathrooms and found a
girl crying there. She was probably twice

my age, I'd guess fifteen or sixteen, but I had no qualms about reaching out to her. I stepped right up and asked her what was wrong, and she told me she was crying over a family problem she was having. I took her hand in mine and looked into her swollen eyes. "If you'll give your heart to Jesus and trust Him, He will help you," I said. "I can pray with you if you'd like." So we stood right there, blocking the bathroom stalls, and I led that teenage girl to a relationship with God. When it was over, I could hardly wait to tell Papa what I'd done. He was so proud of me for witnessing to that girl. He said I was a natural to follow in his footsteps one day. For a long time, I thought so, too.

Papa took turns taking Charity, Cameron, and me with him on his travels, but I went the most often, probably because I was the oldest and the assumed heir apparent to the ministry. I saw more of the country before I turned ten than most people see in their lifetime. By the time I was eleven or twelve I was flying by myself to meet Papa at the venues where he was ministering.

I loved being in airports, and I learned early on that they're great places for witnessing. I picked my subjects randomly. One way we were taught was to close our eyes and choose a color — mine was usually yellow — then open our eyes and witness to the first person we saw who was wearing it. Most people were nice enough, or at least they tolerated me for a couple of minutes before rushing off to catch a plane (or so they said).

Then I learned from Papa that the best time for evangelizing wasn't *in* the airport, but on the plane, because people couldn't get away from me there, at least not for however long we were in the air. I usually took advantage of those first moments after the plane reaches altitude and everyone sighs a breath of relief and settles in. I knew the drill, because Papa had taught me well. My sales pitch was based on the argument made by the Greek philosopher Aristotle twenty-three hundred years ago that there are three basic tenets of persuasion to win someone over to your way of thinking. The first is ethos, or establishing credibility with your chosen subject, which is followed by pathos, or making an emotional connection with the subject. Then comes logos, or going in for the kill by making your case and being prepared to back up what you're saying. Papa trained my siblings and me with challenges. One was that we'd be given an object, it could be anything, and we competed to see who could evangelize best using it as a prop.

I got so good, or at least so I thought, that I could start the conversation with something as benign as a pencil. "Gosh," I'd say, rolling a yellow No. 2 between my forefinger and my thumb. "The pencil is an amazing invention, don't you think?" My seatmate would always take the bait and answer with a nod or a smile, just enough of an opening for me to be able to continue my pitch. "We've been so overtaken with technology over the years that we seem to have forgotten how to write our thoughts out," I'd say. "And, you know, I feel like I have a lot to write about." I'd wait a second or two for the inevitable question from my seatmate. *Like what?* That's when I knew I'd hooked them. I'd then launch into a spiritual experience I'd had — a God Moment. After that, it was time to reel them in: logos. The dictionary definition is "the Word of God, made incarnate in Jesus Christ." Most times, people listened politely as I explained the way to salvation and recited some Bible verses to back up my position — that the difference between being swooped up to Heaven and doomed to Hell was as simple as the act of accepting Christ as the savior. As it said in Romans 10:9–10, *"That if you confess with your mouth, 'Jesus is Lord,' and believe in your heart that God raised him from the dead, you will be saved. For it is with your heart that you believe and are justified, and it is with your mouth that you confess and are saved."* My efforts were usually met with some kind of praise about my commitment, as well as my knowledge of the Good Book. *Ah, what a precocious kid.* Remember, I was an adolescent, and I knew the Bible better than most of the adults.

After a while, witnessing became a game to me. I remember this one time. I was seated next to this guy, a philosopher. I was on the aisle side, and he had the window seat. The plane reached altitude, and I started with my pencil teaser. He seemed half-willing to play the game. But by the time I got to the logos part of my pitch, about halfway through the two-hour flight, he had had enough. Judging from the grimace on his face, he was clearly becoming irritated with the pesky kid seated beside him. He flat-out ignored me, staring out the window, pretending to read his newspaper, or studying the safety card. I knew he was fed up with the game, and he clearly didn't want to play anymore. Did that stop me? Uh-uh. It made me more determined. Unabashed, I continued my pitch. In my head I was thinking, *Heh heh heh. I'm going to get this guy.* Translation: *I'm going to win this game.* I gave it my best shot. In fact, looking back, I was absolutely obnoxious in my quest to win him over. It was like Chinese poke torture. I kept poking him with all of my religious fervor. I wouldn't stop proselytizing. It got to the point where he was squirming in his seat and gritting his teeth, and I loved it. "Well, I appreciate what you're saying, but I don't agree," he said. To which I smugly replied: "And just because you don't agree doesn't mean it's not true." I was a serious evangelical kid, and I took myself way too seriously.

When the plane landed, the philosopher nearly knocked over other passengers to get away from me. I didn't care that he was annoyed; I had done what I was supposed to do. Even if it hadn't led him to a breakthrough moment, I had done what God (and Papa) expected of me. If the man chose not to be saved, it was his bum in the fire, not mine.

# 3
## YOUNG EVANGELIST

Let eloquence be flung to the dogs rather than souls be lost. What we want is to win souls. They are not won by flowery speeches.

— CHARLES SPURGEON,
*SERMONS ON PROVERBS*

You know the expression Army brat? There's a whole blog about it where people complete the sentence: "You know you're an Army brat if." You know you're an Army brat if: "You learned your alphabet as 'Alpha, Bravo, Charlie.' " "Your accent changes to fit in a new geographical location." "Your father comes into the bedroom at 0455 hours and turns on the light; comes back at 0500 hours and turns over the bunks." And so on.

Well you know you're an evangelical brat if: You believe that the Bible is the inerrant word of God. (I did my best to imagine

Lot's wife literally turning into a pillar of salt.) You pray daily every day, and then some, about anything and everything because nothing is too big or too small for God. You know that the most famous musician in the Bible, King David, used music for worshipping God, and you avoid secular music in favor of Christian songs. You don't take up the vices of the devil, like smoking or drugs or drinking. Above all, you share your faith and enlist others to get "saved" because the alternative is so frightening.

You've earned the title of mega evangelical brat when you've spread the word of God to people on six continents, hung out with Christian giants Oral Roberts, Joyce Meyer, and Jimmy Swaggart, played Jesus on a mission trip to India, and witnessed to a stadium of ten thousand screaming teens before you've turned ten years old.

That'd be me.

It was my father's idea to get me out onstage with him at his Christian youth rallies, a combination religious revival and rock concert called "Acquire the Fire" because the idea is to get kids "on fire" for Jesus. Papa is a superstar in the charismatic Christian world. Every year, he packs stadiums and coliseums in major cities across the country with his appearances. I grew up attending them. I hadn't even been to school yet the first time he invited my younger sister, Charity, and me to come onstage and belt out our favorite Christian song at the Mabee Center in Tulsa. Our little-girl voices were squeaky and out of tune (way out of tune), but we knew every word, and I even slapped my thigh to the beat. The crowd went wild for us. *"My God is big enough; my God is big enough; My God is big enough for every situation."*

Once, I got up the nerve to preface our song with one of my favorite scriptures, Ephesians 4:29–32: "Do not let any unwholesome talk come out of your mouths, but only what is helpful for building others up according to their needs, that it may benefit those who listen. And do not grieve the Holy Spirit of God, with whom you were sealed for the day of redemption. Get rid of all bitterness, rage and anger, brawling and slander, along with every form of malice. Be kind and compassionate to one another, forgiving each other, just as in Christ God forgave you." Papa was so proud. "That's the first time she's ever done that in front of anybody," he said. "Amen!" Those little performances were kind of fearsome for such a little kid, but at least I had Charity's hand to hold on to. And, I have to admit, as much as I suffered from stage fright, I kind of liked the attention — as long as my sister was by my side.

But the first time I had to go it alone was a different story. I nearly threw up backstage while I waited for Papa to introduce me. We were at the Denver Coliseum, and the place was filled to capacity with ten-thousand-plus teens who were on fire for Jesus. I wasn't quite a teenager yet, but I had big news to share with my Christian peers. Papa had always put a lot of pressure on us to start thinking about what we wanted to do with our lives. So, when, at the age of twelve, I decided to build my own website for God, he wanted the world to know.

What I'd done was really quite an accomplishment. The idea came to me one day while I was at home, searching on the computer for God sites. I couldn't find anything for kids my age, which surprised and frustrated me. I was so disappointed that, all on my own, I searched for and employed a web designer to teach me how to build my very own God site. The designer came to our house once or twice a week for several weeks until I got the gist of what I was doing. Papa footed the bill, and I designed and launched the site.

I called it "Girls for God." It had a pink

background with yellow borders, and it was divided into sections on Christian bands and clubs, overseas missions, health and beauty, and, of course, boys. In the middle of the site was an "Ask Hannah" column where preteens and teens were invited to write in with questions about everything from religion and the Bible to hair and makeup tips. My first post about fashion was adorned with a little red lipstick icon and a quotation from Papa, who always said, "Makeup is to highlight your natural beauty, not to cover up your natural ugliness." Ironically, I knew less about how to be fashionable than most other people my age because I was so sheltered and isolated from my generation, but I sure knew plenty about God.

My section "On Getting Saved" got a lot of traffic. I posted the Salvation Prayer there. *"Dear God, I am a sinner and need forgiveness. I believe that Jesus Christ died for my sins. I am willing to turn from sin and invite Jesus to come into my heart as my personal Savior. Amen."* The one called "More about God" was a channel for me to give more advice, and I took it seriously. One of the first questions I got was, "Do all dogs go to Heaven?" I spent hours leafing through books and the Bible looking for sourcing. Finally, I wrote: "In the Bible it talks about how people have spirits, and while our physical bodies don't go to Heaven our spiritual bodies do. Because dogs don't have spirits, or rather, it's not clear in the Bible whether they do, my answer is that they're harmless and loving creatures, so why wouldn't they go to Heaven?" It was only years later I learned that my Christian friends had fed me the dog questions — as well as many others — and then cackled amongst themselves over my fraught but earnest answers.

Papa was so proud of my initiative he insisted I share the website with his followers. I thought that was cool. He was pleased with me, and I loved having his approval.

My debut was in Denver, and I spent hours getting myself ready for my big night. In the hotel that morning, I styled my hair in zigzags, separated the pieces with little butterfly barrettes, and clipped on a pair of my mother's shiny hoop earrings. I pulled on my favorite bright orange top and matched it with a woven orange necklace I'd gotten during a mission trip to Africa. I sprinkled my arms with sparkles, and then brushed each of my eyelids with a wisp of white eye shadow from Mom's makeup bag. I wondered how many boys in the audience would think I was cute.

Backstage, I paced the floor, waiting for Papa to introduce me. I was a ball of nerves. What if I messed up? What if I slipped in my new platform shoes? What if the cat got my tongue and I couldn't speak? I'd prepared some notes, just in case I forgot what I was supposed to say. Waiting and worrying, I read them, over and over, until I thought I knew them by heart. But how would I do, out there, with a blinding spotlight shining in my eyes and ten thousand teenagers watching me?

*If I do this right,* I said to myself, *I could change the world for my generation and maybe even make an impression on Danny Brenner.* Danny was a Messianic Jewish kid whose parents worked for Papa's ministry. He was scrawny, with spiky hair, and he wore diamond studs in his ears. I thought he was the bee's knees. We played chess together occasionally, and I had a secret crush on him. Knowing he could be in the audience made me even more jittery. *Maybe I can pretend I'm sick and back out,* I thought, just before one of the stagehands whispered to me that Papa was nearly ready.

I heard him wrapping up a prayer and knew I was next. "When you leave here you have to have a plan," Papa said softly into the microphone. "How are you going to use your strength and your energy for God? Let me just give you an example tonight.

"A twelve-year-old girl gets an idea. She thinks it's from God. 'What can I do this year to make a difference?' she asks herself. 'Hey! What if I could put a website together that could help other teenage girls and preteen girls to get on fire for God?' So she began working — this was just a few months ago — putting all the material together, and just this week rolled out a webpage for young girls to get on fire for God! In fact, this young lady happens to be my oldest daughter, Hannah Luce. Hannah! Would you come out here?"

I walked onstage, and a spotlight followed me to my place next to Papa. I could see pride written all over his face. That was what mattered most to me, Papa's approval. "Tell the people what you've done," Papa said, handing his microphone over to me.

My voice was a Minnie Mouse trill, a sort of chirpy falsetto. "Well, um, the idea came to me, um, I was looking around, searching the web, and I couldn't find any godly websites for preteens and teens, and that's when the idea hit me. God just struck me in the heart! I just had this desire to make my own website for God. So I went for it!"

The more I talked, the more I relaxed. *There are probably a lot of cute boys in the audience and they're all watching me,* I thought. I felt so important, so accepted. "It was God working through me," I said. "If He can use me, he can use every single one of you!"

The more I talked, the more settled my nerves became. The audience cheered me on. They liked me! They really liked me! I didn't need my notes anymore. I was on a roll. "And I just encourage you to open up your heart this weekend and for the rest of your life, just to really listen to God and what He has to say," I said. "There are people who have just given their lives to Jesus. This is designed to help those people to be more of a Girl of God."

I had spoken longer than I'd ever intended, but no one seemed bored or in a rush for me to leave, and that felt kind of nice.

"So," I said, wrapping up somewhat abruptly, "I hope you have a great night, and . . . God Bless You!"

When I finished, Papa swept me up in his arms for thousands of teens to see. His eyes were alight with pride, and he had a huge grin on his face. He puffed up his chest, gave me a big kiss on the cheek, and I twirled around in my pretty platform shoes and ran as fast as I could offstage. As I ran, I heard Papa say, "That's my girl! That's my firstborn! Hannah Luce!" The kids in the audience whooped and hollered.

It was the most proud of me I would ever feel Papa was.

I was twelve years old.

# 4
## AFRICA

And these signs shall follow them that believe; In my name shall they cast out devils; they shall speak with new tongues;

They shall take up serpents; and if they drink any deadly thing, it shall not hurt them; they shall lay hands on the sick, and they shall recover.

— MARK 16:17–18

I took my first steps in an African jungle. By the time I was ten, I'd traveled to every state in the country to spread the word of God. By high school I'd talked Him up to people on six continents. My parents could have named their ministry "Missions R Us." We were always on the road looking for people to save. A lot of those mission trips were overseas to remote villages at the ends of the earth where people had never even heard about Jesus and the Bible, but that was the point of our being there. It wasn't just Americans who needed saving, although our youth were being lost to what Papa called "virtue terrorists, the purveyors of popular culture." Papa said people all over the world were in danger of languishing for all of eternity in Hell because, through no fault of their own, they didn't even know the name Jesus. It was up to people like us to reach as many people like them as we possibly could.

I loved taking mission trips overseas. The more uncivilized or culturally foreign the land was, the more I wanted to be there. The hardships we encountered on those trips were well worth the experience I got from them. I was just a little girl when I saw my mother and a group of team leaders from the ministry pray over a frail-looking woman living in India to command the demons to leave her body. My parents were always encountering people with demons, and both are very capable of confronting evil spirits.

I remember that on one of our trips to a remote village in Africa, my sister looked at a woman and cried, "She has red eyes! She has red eyes!" She claimed the woman was trying to engage her using silent manner-isms. I didn't see any red in the woman's eyes, but I knew we didn't have to worry

53

about catching her demons because we had Jesus in our hearts.

Returning to life as usual after those missions was tough, but there was always the next adventure to look forward to. A couple of years after the trip to east Africa, I rode for four hours in a canoe, in alligator-infested waters, to reach natives in the jungles of Panama. I've played with monkeys in Tanzania, ridden elephants in Thailand, danced with warriors from the Maasai tribe in Kenya, and visited Buddhist and Hindu temples in India to observe their religious practices and pray that I might one day have an opportunity to persuade them to see things our way — to become one of us. One of the high points of the India trip was putting on a drama of the life and death and resurrection of Jesus, and I got to play Jesus on the cross.

But my most memorable trip was to a place in South Africa called Harrismith, a shantytown about two and a half hours through mountainous terrain from Johannesburg. Some thirty-five thousand people lived there, most of them in abject poverty. The language was native South African Sesotho, and many of the people still relied on witch doctors to cure them of sickness and cleanse them of evil spirits. The region was predominantly Christian, but Islam was fast gaining a foothold in many of the poorer black communities, mostly for its emphasis on charity and social reform, but also because of a radical rejection by blacks of the Christian-based society that had permitted the tragedy of Apartheid. It was not an easy audience for us, but challenges never stopped a good evangelical Christian from his work.

We spent a month in Harrismith, camping on nearby safari land where gazelles and zebra grazed. I woke up every morning before sunrise to read Bible verses and watch the sun turn red, orange, and gold as it came up above the horizon. We started out early every day and did most of our work on the edges of the city, where there seemed to be nothing but rows of tiny, broken-down houses. There were thirty of us on that mission and plenty of neighborhoods to hit, so we split into teams of five, each with a translator, and walked from one rundown shack to the next, knocking on doors with messages from the Lord.

Neither language nor cultural barriers gave us pause. We had a system for most any situation, and this was no exception. The first step was to ingratiate ourselves at each stop by offering to do odd jobs for the homeowner or tenant. "Hi! We're from America!" I'd say. "We came here to help. Is there anything we can do to help you?" The task could be sweeping, chopping wood, preparing food, or washing clothes, pretty much any kind of household chore. People were usually leery of our offer at first. You could see the question in their expressions: *What's the catch?* But most of them accepted.

One of our first jobs was helping a family prepare for a funeral. A funeral was a decadent ritual in Africa. People dressed in colorful, native costumes, and the host family, the bereaved, prepared a feast big enough to feed everyone who came. While the cooks prepared dishes like Bobotie (lamb casserole) and Geel Rys (yellow rice) with Blatjang (apricot and raisin chutney) and Komkomer Sambal (cucumber relish), my job was to help make a traditional beer they call Umqombothi. Making the beer involved stirring a mixture of malt, maize, yeast, and water in a cast-iron vat (a potjie) and simmering it over a fire outside the house. The finished brew was a fermented mash of stuff with a sickening sour smell, which was then strained and poured into a communal drum they called a "gogogo." Once the brew cooled, it was finally ready for sharing. I could hardly handle the gigantic wooden stick I used to stir, and the smell almost made me sick, but I still had fun.

Some of the jobs we did were short, and others took hours. We worked however long it took to get it finished and then proceeded to step two, which was, you guessed it: the pitch. "Now that we've done this for you, would you do something in return and listen to our story?" People were so gracious; they almost always did. We figured if it took a special tactic to give people the chance to be saved, so be it.

Our pitch was right out of the Evangelism Explosion Workbook. The goal was to get others to recite the Salvation Prayer. We started off with a deck of colored flash cards that showed the way to salvation with a story: the rainbow colors that lead to Jesus. The first was a picture of a boy with the black heart of a sinner. The red card represented the blood of Jesus when he died for our sins. The blue card symbolized baptism, and the white card showed the boy acknowledging his sin and praying for forgiveness, just as David did in Psalm 51: "Wash and I shall be whiter than snow." The final two cards were green, symbolizing growth, or discipleship. And, finally, gold, which stood for the crown God brings you in heaven for being faithful to His command. (As a kid I was taught that for everything I did for God I'd get a jewel in my crown, and I always worried when I did something wrong that I'd end up with a light crown.)

The goal was that, after every time we told the story, we tried to get someone to recite the Salvation Prayer. "Dear God, I am a sinner and need forgiveness. I believe that Jesus Christ died for my sins. I am willing to turn from sin and invite Jesus to come into my heart as my personal Savior. Amen." I always elaborated. "I want you to change my world. I want you to help me stand strong against the enemy. To help me to see through your eyes, to speak to me in my greatest hour of need. I want for you to be my all. I want for you to be my everything. Please forgive me for my sins. I need you, Jesus. I need you to help me stand strong. Amen."

Some days went better than others, and every night, when our work was done, we returned to camp and tallied up how many people each of the groups had saved that day. It was a pretty competitive process, and I loved winning. Papa always said that if I wasn't looking hard enough, someone wouldn't get saved, and God would hold me responsible. I knew what that meant, so I'd trained my eye really well. But, one day, toward the end of our stay, I did almost miss someone.

My team and I walked into a dusty little courtyard, toward a cluster of tiny houses. A man was sitting on a rock outside one of the houses, and he was bathing himself from a pail with about two inches of muddy water in the bottom and a bar of pink soap. The man didn't look up, and we nearly passed by him. He seemed indifferent, and it looked as if he was alone at the house. We were about to move on when I told the group to stop — we needed to get our numbers up. After praying so hard every day I felt like I was in tune with what God wanted for our team, and He wanted us to talk to that man.

The man was a little bit stout, with a potbelly, probably sixty or seventy, though he looked much older. He had sharp facial features and a long hooked nose. He was hunched over, washing himself. His cane was propped up against the rock. I was pretty sensitive about being intrusive, but I knew it was my duty, my obligation, to get his attention.

I was thirteen, and everyone in my group was older than me, all of them fourteen or fifteen or sixteen years old, and our team leader was eighteen, but I took the lead. I walked up to the man, and he still didn't look up.

"My name is Hannah," I said. "What's your name?"

The man didn't answer, so I had all of the others on our team introduce themselves as well.

He still didn't speak.

"Can we pray for you for anything?" I asked.

The man shook his head. No.

"Please," I said. "There must be something we can pray over you for."

The man started shouting in Zulu. "Ndiyekele! Ndiyekele!" What is he saying? I asked the translator. She told us the man was blind and hard of hearing. He wanted us to leave him alone. I wanted to leave. I wanted to move on to the next house, where there were more people to save. People who were bound to be more open than the man washing himself on the rock. But then I remembered Papa's words. "If you see an opportunity to pray over someone and you don't, you miss what God is saying to you." I felt compelled to pray for the man's eyes. In my mind, I was thinking about the story in the Book of John in the Bible when Jesus made the blind man see.

As Jesus was walking along, he saw a man who had been blind from birth. "Rabbi," his disciples asked him, "why was this man born blind? Was it because of his own sins or his parents' sins?"

"It was not because of his sins or his parents' sins," Jesus answered. "This happened so the power of God could be seen in him. We must quickly carry out the tasks assigned us by the one who sent us. The night is coming, and then no one can work. But while I am here in the world, I am the light of the world."

Then he spat on the ground, made mud with the saliva, and spread the mud over the blind man's eyes. He told him, "Go wash yourself in the pool of Siloam." So the man went and washed and came back seeing!

His neighbors and others who knew him as a blind beggar asked each other, "Isn't this the man who used to sit and beg?" Some said he was, and others said, "No, he just looks like him!"

But the beggar kept saying, "Yes, I am the same one!"

They asked, "Who healed you? What happened?"

He told them, "The man they call Jesus made mud and spread it over my eyes and told me, 'Go to the pool of Siloam and wash yourself.' So I went and washed, and now I can see!"

I knew what I had to do. I didn't have dirt to make mud, but I knew God allowed us to ad lib in situations like this, so I decided to use the soap instead. "I think God wants us to do this," I said. The man didn't understand, but he nodded his head in agreement. I removed his thick glasses. Everyone began praying, and I took the soap and began washing the man's eyes. I kept telling myself to believe. The Bible told me if I believed hard enough — if I believed that the man would see — then God would make it so.

We continued praying for the man and, after a few minutes, he looked straight into my eyes. His eyes got really big, and he began mumbling in his native tongue. "What is he saying?" I asked the interpreter. "He's saying 'I can see! I can see!' " she said. I turned back to the man and saw a sense of awe in his expression as he studied me. I felt as if he were studying every angle and crevice of my face. I looked into his eyes. They were black and empty. I felt like I was looking into a dark, bottomless well. Could he really see? Why would he pretend?

I decided to push God a little harder. "May we pray over your ears?" I asked. The man eagerly agreed. After we'd been praying awhile, the translator leaned over and whispered something in the man's ear. The man whispered back. "He can hear!" the translator shouted. "He can hear!" Before that, when the man said he was hard of hearing, the translator had been shouting in his ear, but he could barely hear her. Now he heard her speaking in a faint whisper. We all cried "Hallelujah!"

We weren't finished yet. We asked the man to join us for services at the local church on Sunday. He said he would, except that he had hurt his leg and had trouble walking because he was in so much pain. I began to pray over his leg. I was praying and praying, yet nothing was happening. *How can this be?* I wondered. *Why would God stop responding to our prayers now?* The translator began speaking to the man with a sharp tongue. It was clear that they were arguing. "What's wrong?" I asked. "What's going on?"

The translator pointed to the man's wrist. "The bracelet!" she said. "He told me it's from a witch doctor, and I'm trying to get him to take it off." The witch doctor had told the man the bracelet would help to ease his leg pain, and he refused to take it off.

My team members and I had been taught

that certain symbols meant evil spirits were present and that the spirits could control anything. For instance, a voodoo doll has an evil spirit living inside that can come upon you, but if you get rid of the doll, you're released from the grasp of the bad spirit. Was the bracelet the reason God wasn't answering our prayers over the man's leg? My team members and I agreed that it could be the problem.

Buoyed by my previous success, I waved away the translator and put my hands over the man's hands. "Please," I said, gently. "Please allow me to remove your bracelet." The man hesitated. "Please," I said. "Please just take it off. Take it off and believe in our God. Believe that our God will take away your pain." Slowly, with shaking hands, the man removed the bracelet. We all prayed over him for relief of the pain in his leg, even harder than we'd prayed about his eyes and his ears.

Soon the man said his leg didn't hurt anymore. I could hardly believe it myself. First his eyes, then his ears, and now his leg. By then, it was getting dark, and we had to head back to camp. There hadn't been time to take out our cards and try to get him to recite the Salvation Prayer. I promised the man we would return in the morning to see how he was feeling. "Please," I said. "Please don't put that bracelet back on."

My team and I were giddy on the way back to camp. We certainly weren't going to win that night's contest for saves since we had spent the whole day with that one man and had run out of time to witness to him. But there was always tomorrow.

After dinner, we told the other teams about what had happened with the old man. "Praise God!" everyone said.

I tossed and turned all that night, worrying that if the man put that bracelet on again and died before we got back to try to save him in the morning, he would go to Hell.

When we returned the next day, on a Sunday, the man wasn't there. I was both disappointed and scared. Disappointed because I wanted to see if the miracle had stuck. Scared, thinking about the power of God. I couldn't get the man out of my mind after that. I couldn't help but wonder what had become of him. Could he still see? Hear? Had he put the bracelet back on?

We were working in different neighborhoods, but I finally made it back to his house a day or two later. Once again, he wasn't there. We asked around about the man with the hunched back, and people told us that he could still see and hear.

And the reason he wasn't home was that he had gone to the Christian church nearby. And he had *walked* there.

Wow, I thought. We had assisted God with a miracle. It was the first time in my life that I really felt worthy of being the kid of Ron Luce. Maybe I did have the Luce juice.

# 5
## BAD BOOKS

I have no Faith — I dare not utter the words & thoughts that crowd in my heart — & make me suffer untold agony.

— MOTHER TERESA,
IN AN UNDATED LETTER, IN
*COME BE MY LIGHT: THE PRIVATE*
*WRITINGS OF THE "SAINT OF CALCUTTA"*

It wasn't long after my big debut at "Acquire the Fire," Papa's big event in Denver, that I began to really question the beliefs I was raised with. As little as I knew about life, having been so sheltered in the cloistered evangelical world I lived in, I had been taught that contentment was mine as long as I continued to follow God's commands. The only problem was, I was having trouble hearing Him, and that caused me to feel cut off and isolated from everything and everyone I knew.

I didn't dare tell my parents that I feared

God had abandoned me. Papa said that God had expectations of us and if we paid attention we'd just know what those expectations were. I kept praying for hints about what He wanted of me, but I wasn't getting any feedback. I'd begun feeling anxious, wondering if I'd done or said something to incur His wrath. I tried to hide my anxiety from my parents. At first I figured, why worry them? God was bound to get back to me at some point. But as hard as I prayed to get His attention, it just wasn't happening. I was doing plenty of talking, but He wasn't talking back, and I started worrying about Papa and Mom finding out. They wouldn't understand if they knew my dilemma and, even worse, they would fear for me, fear that by having lost that relationship I was condemned to spend eternity with the damned, wailing and gnashing my teeth in a fiery Hell. I knew too much of what the Bible said for my own good. I'd studied it since the time I could read. The Book of John says, "My sheep listen to my voice; I know them, and they follow me. I give them eternal life, and they shall never perish." Papa always said the way to know we belong to God is to hear His voice, to know when He is speaking to us. But I couldn't and I didn't.

I prayed for guidance. For hours on end, I sat on the floor in my bedroom, with my door locked, praying for Him to help me understand what was happening to me. Praying for Him to explain why I felt so abandoned and alone because I couldn't *hear* Him. "O Lord God," I prayed. "I know you've got a plan for me, or at least that's what everybody says. I just need to figure out what it is. I'm doing everything I know to do to figure it out, but it seems as though the more I try to understand, the less You speak to me. Lord God, are You testing me? Yes, that's it. It must be a test."

When I still didn't hear back, I began looking for answers to my questions in books that I secretly collected from the kids I called silent rebels in Papa's ministry. The silent rebels were a small, anonymous group within the Teen Mania family who were creative and artsy, as well as better-read and better-dressed than the rest of us. The names and faces changed, but there were always a handful of them among the hundreds of teenagers who were on campus at any given time, either interning or attending Christian boot camp, although Papa never knew who they were. Like everyone else who came to Teen Mania, they were there as a show of their devotion to God, but they were different in that they didn't have blind faith in the word of the Gospel. I thought they were really cool, and I secretly related more to them than I did to the others. So I started seeking the truth, as they did, in places other than the Bible and the books sanctioned by Teen Mania as appropriate reading for us.

I'd collected dozens of books and hidden them in my room. I could hardly wait for nighttime and the lights to go out in the house so I could lock my door and begin sifting through them.

One night, long after my parents had gone to bed, I was in my room, at the other end of our rambling house, listening to a book on tape that I had gotten from one of my silent rebel friends and started the day before. *The Great Divorce* is a theological fantasy written by C. S. Lewis, a sort of Kafkaesque portrayal of the afterlife. Intellectually, it was way over my head, but that didn't stop me from trying to understand it.

The gist of the story is this: The narrator finds himself stuck in a gray, joyless city. He and a group of others eventually board a bus that travels to the foothills of an idyllic paradise where shining men and women meet them, people they once knew from earth. It turns out the bus passengers are "ghosts" from Hell, and the shiny men and women are "spirits" from Heaven who offer to show them the way in. But, rather than accepting the spirits' offer of a chance at repentance and, ultimately, the great rewards of Heaven, almost all of the passengers choose to return to their grim, gloomy city, or Hell. The message of the book is that we decide to live in Hell by making choices that exclude us from finding in life the infinite happiness, or Heaven, that God wants for us. I couldn't get enough of it.

That night, though, as I listened for any sounds of my parents with one ear, and the narrator on the tape with the other, I heard the part of the story where a ghost tells a spirit, *"I wish I had never been born. What are we born for?" she asks. "For infinite happiness," the spirit replies. "You can step out into it at any moment."* When I heard that, something stirred in me, and I suddenly felt terrified. I felt like that doomed ghost on the tape. *Had I ever felt infinite happiness?* I asked myself. No, I admitted. I hadn't. I had felt merry, and silly, and cheerful, but never completely joyful or content. I had always been taught that God was infinite and that, if only I accepted Him, eternal happiness was mine. But if Lewis was right,

I had to make my own happiness, to choose it, and I had no idea how to do that. Did what he wrote in *The Great Divorce* mean my parents' definition of God — what I had been taught since I was able to comprehend words and thoughts — was wrong?

Suddenly I was overcome with feelings of panic. My skin prickled, as though my nerve endings were on fire, and my perspiration-soaked hair stuck to the nape of my neck. My heart was banging in my chest. Trying to calm myself, I recited aloud a Bible verse I had learned as a very young child: "God works all things for good for those who love Him and are called according to His purposes." I loved God. At least I was trying to love Him, this mysterious entity that left so many people, including my parents, with lingering feelings of joy and fullness that I knew nothing about.

I began crying and shaking. "God!" I prayed, curling up in a ball in the corner of my room. "Where are you? Why have you abandoned me? I'm just a kid. Why do I feel so alone in all of this? Why do I feel trapped in the gray city? Why can't I hear you? *I'm so confused!*"

My body trembled, and I couldn't breathe. I looked at the clock on my nightstand. It was three-thirty in the morning. My parents always taught us that unless blood, smoke, or fire were involved, we were not to wake them after bedtime, and I knew that if I did awaken them I'd be punished for staying up so late on a school night. I was too panicked, too distraught to care. As far as I was concerned, this was as much of an emergency as a fire.

"I need Papa!" I cried. "Papa! Papa?"

I left my bedroom and slowly made my way through the dark corridor to the other end of the house where my parents' room was. I cracked open the door and quietly slipped inside, hoping not to wake my mother. I tiptoed to Papa's side of the bed and nudged him. At first he didn't stir. "Papa!" I cried, shaking him. "Papa! Please, Papa! Help me! I'm afraid! I don't know what to believe anymore!" Tears streamed down my cheeks, and I was panting and sobbing.

Papa shot up in bed. "What is it, Hannah?" he asked. "What is it, sweetheart?" I began to wail. "Shhhhhhhhh!" Papa whispered, climbing out of bed and ushering me out of the room.

"Princess! Princess, tell me what happened!" he said when we were outside in the hallway. Papa had called me princess for as long as I could remember.

"I don't know what to do anymore!" I said, weeping uncontrollably. "I was . . . reading . . . books . . . I can't . . . God . . . how can I?" I was barely able to choke my words out. "The ghost . . . the ghh-hooosssstttt!"

"What are you talking about?" Papa asked. All I could do was point toward my room and blather incoherently.

"Show me," Papa said.

I led him to my room where my boom box was still playing the book on tape. *Friend, I am not suggesting at all. You see, I know now. Let us be frank. Our opinions were not honestly come by. We simply found ourselves in contact with a certain current of ideas and plunged into it because it seemed modern and successful. At college, you know, we just started automatically writing the kind of essays that got good marks and saying the kind of things that won applause. When, in our whole lives, did we honestly face, in solitude, the one question on which all turned: whether after all the Supernatural might not in fact occur? When did we put up one moment's real resistance to the loss of our faith?*

Papa turned off the boom box. My other secret books were spread out on the floor next to my bed, all of them with the same theme — re-examining evangelical Christian dogma, defining a different kind of God than my father's God. All of the books were open to different pages. The little princess had obviously been reading for quite some time. Among the book were *Blue Like Jazz: Nonreligious Thoughts on Christian Spirituality* and *Prayer and the Art of Volkswagen Maintenance,* both by Donald Miller, and *Lifelines: Holding On (And Letting Go),* by Forrest Church.

I thought Papa would be mad at me, but he wasn't at all. He took it all in for a moment, then sat me down on the bed. His eyes were kind and concerned. "What are you doing up so late?" he asked.

I was shaking so hard I couldn't answer. I just sobbed.

"You don't need to be reading these," Papa said, kneeling on the floor and closing each of my books.

He gathered up my books — my treasures — and tucked them under his arm. "Tonight, go to sleep," he said gently, walking toward the door, "and we'll talk about this in the morning."

"Wait," I said boldly, if sheepishly.

Papa stopped and turned toward me. I could see the concern on his face. I knew I had disappointed him.

"What are you going to do with my

books?" I asked.

"It's only for a night," Papa said, reassuring me. "It's time to go to bed now."

So I obeyed. I put my head on the pillow and I went to sleep, exhausted from my angst.

The next morning, early, Papa came into my room and woke me up for school. I was still wiping sleep from my eyes when he handed me a book. "This is for you," he said, smiling.

I looked at the cover of the book: *I Am Not But I Know I Am: Welcome to the Story of God.* I cracked it open and skimmed the first few pages.

*". . . this book is not about you and making your story better, but about waking up to the infinitely bigger God Story happening all around you, and God's invitation to you to join Him in it."*

I closed the book and looked at Papa, who was looking at me expectantly. What did he want me to say?

"You don't need to be reading any of those other books," Papa said, looking down at me, his smile reassuring. "It will only confuse you. When you have questions, ask me."

"Yes sir," I said, my heart sinking.

I didn't ask about the books he had taken

from me the night before. I knew I'd never see them again.

# 6
## BIBLE BOOT CAMP

Belief compelled through fear is not belief,
it is blind and forced obedience.
> — CARLTON D. PEARSON,
> *GOD IS NOT A CHRISTIAN, NOR A JEW,*
> *MUSLIM, HINDU. . . . GOD DWELLS*
> *WITH US, IN US, AROUND US, AS US*

It was that summer, as I was about to turn fourteen, that Papa sent me to Bible Boot Camp in Chattanooga. I'm certain the reason was that he thought I needed fixing. It's not like I objected to going to boot camp. In fact, when he said he thought it would be a good idea for me to go, I said I thought he was probably right. Maybe if I made an extra effort, and went willingly, God would reward me with his voice.

"When do I go?" I asked.

I knew I was broken even better than Papa did. How could I not? I was still borrowing books from the silent rebels, only I was hiding them better now. Not only that, I'd even begun pulling forbidden titles off the shelves of the local library and stealing away to a quiet corner to read them. Whenever the librarian came by, I covered whatever I was reading with one of my schoolbooks. When I was finished, I'd tuck whatever book it was back on the shelf so no one would ever know. The more I read, the more questions I had, the more confused I became, the more I felt like a foreigner in my own body. Something was obviously terribly wrong with me. There had to be. I prayed harder than ever for something from God, some word, some sound, acknowledgment of my struggle, but nothing came. I strained so hard to hear my ears throbbed and my head ached. I began to fear that maybe it wasn't my hearing after all. Maybe my hearing was perfectly okay — tiptop — but God just wasn't talking to me. The thought of that was even more troubling. It was devastating. Why didn't He like me? He clearly didn't have any problem with anyone else I knew. Mom and Papa had conversations with Him all the time, as did my siblings and our friends and literally thousands of kids I'd met (and some I'd even evangelized to) through Teen Mania — except, of course, that small group of silent rebels.

Papa would have worried for their souls had he known they were seeking answers in places other than the scriptures. Their secret was safe with me. No way I was going to out any of them.

I had begun collecting my own secrets. Plenty of them. Some seemed pretty silly. Why couldn't I admit I had begun smudging on lip gloss when I wasn't home? Some were serious secrets. What would Papa have said if he knew I was secretly questioning whether my life here was even worth living? I had been raised with the very Gnostic philosophy that I was only living in this evil, materialistic world to be able to share my knowledge of the word of God with the many lost souls on this earth. My job as God's servant was to save as many of them as I could from a forbidding fiery Hell, the place of eternal suffering, where everyone spent their days in misery. *(So shall it be at the end of the world: the angels shall come forth, and sever the wicked from among the just, And shall cast them into the furnace of fire: there shall be wailing and gnashing of teeth. Matthew 13:49–50.)* I was taught my body was nothing more than a temporary cover (not to mention a hindrance, because it exposed me to ungodly temptations) while I was here, working as the bearer of

God's word. The spirit is divine and good. The body is earthly and evil. What then, I wondered, was the point of the battle I was in with myself? Was this place even worth my time? If I were an alien from God and not of this earth, why not just commit what I called "Christian suicide"— kill off my body to free up my soul to go to Heaven now? I was already saved, so I didn't have to worry that suicide was a quick ticket to Hell. Did I?

I decided to try boot camp before I took such drastic action.

Papa took me to Tennessee, which meant I got to spend hours of alone time with him. I loved traveling with Papa; it was one of my favorite things to do. When it was just him and me, we'd talk about everything under the sun, and he always made time for us to do something special when we were in a new city — a trip to an amusement park, or a late-night comedy show, or a great burger joint. Driving in the car together was always so much fun. We'd listen to music from Papa's day, and he'd imitate the artists, albeit badly. Between songs, he'd ask me what God had been teaching me lately. I knew I had to have something ready to tell him, and I always did. For instance, I'd say, "God is teaching me to have peace and understanding." Then Papa would ask, "What does that mean to you?" I'd say something like, "Well, I was reading this Bible verse and it really came alive to me because I realized I was being impatient with my sister, Charity, and I need to have peace and trust that God will work all things out for the good." Papa would be satisfied with that answer and go back to singing his songs. I never wanted our car rides to end, and this one was no different.

Once we got to Chattanooga I started getting excited for the new experience I was about to have. Papa was excited for me. I could tell. I made sure I looked my best in my favorite whitewashed flare jeans and blue Hollister hoodie, to impress the other kids. I pulled my hair up in a messy ponytail, which I thought looked really cool. I tucked my lip gloss in my pocket for later, after Papa dropped me off. I was ready to meet the challenge.

I don't know what I was expecting, besides getting to meet Kay Arthur, the evangelical superstar, whose ministry hosted the Bible Boot Camp, but I wasn't prepared for what I found when we got there. As we drove into the campground, I looked around and felt a lump in my throat to match the lump in my stomach. It looked like every other summer camp, not a place where I might get to hear God. I saw cabins on one side for the girls, and cabins on the other side for the boys, and a small, common building in the center. That was where we would spend the majority of our time every day, in that nondescript building. It was where our meals were served and our classes were held. Papa thought it was all just fine, but I hated the set-up. I tried to hide my disappointment and hoped for the best.

Papa left, and I went to my bunk to settle in. I unpacked my things and began leafing through a pack of information on my bed. The top page was a mission statement for the boot camp. "To train Christlike leaders for a generation," it said. Students were guaranteed to leave with "1) an understanding of how to study the Bible for themselves, and, 2) intense worship and challenging messages conveying the power of the Gospel to this generation and God's call on their lives." Our daily activities were to include "Bible study, worship, prayer, sports, and fellowship with teens from around the world," the pamphlet said.

Well, that was sort of true.

As it turned out, there wasn't much else going on besides scripture lessons and exercises, as well as worship and prayer. I couldn't help but think I could have gone across the road from my house in Garden valley to the Teen Mania campus for that. In fact, I had done that for most of my life. If I couldn't hear God in my hometown in Texas, I certainly wasn't going to hear him at camp in Chattanooga. I wouldn't even get to hear Kay Arthur. She was away on a mission trip. So much for positive thinking.

We had somewhere between fifty and a hundred students at camp. That first day set the tone for the entire two weeks: we woke up at eight, grabbed a quick breakfast from a buffet of cereals and juices, then sat at the banquet tables and listened to an hour of what I'd call "ranting scripture" from an angry-sounding manly-looking woman who was supposed to motivate us. We were all given copies of Kay's newest biblical novel, *Israel, My Beloved,* as well as a workbook that turned out to be the heart of the program.

Six hours of classes a day consisted of Bible readings followed by exercises in the workbook. Each of the exercises included reading an assigned scripture and completing an accompanying assignment that reminded me of tick-tack-toe except that it wasn't as stimulating or as much fun. One assignment, for instance, was to read a passage of scripture from the Book of John, then go through the passage and circle all of John's words to Jesus and all of Jesus' words to John and cross-reference them. That was one of the more interesting exercises, and I was so bored that in order to keep from falling asleep I had to talk to my neighbor, a nice girl who had traveled all the way from Japan to be there. I had grown up reading the Bible. I got myself out of bed every day at 5:00 a.m. to make sure I got my scripture readings in. I didn't need to be circling dialogue like some Christian novice.

After a couple of days of those endless classes, I began to feel like a slave to God. "Is this what I have to look forward to for the rest of my life?" I wondered. By the third day, when everyone else was circling whatever it was the workbook instructed us to do, I just drew circles. Endless circles. Tiny, tiny circles, all over the page. Thousands of them, each one connected to the next. When one page was full, I turned to the next and did the same thing. I'm sure my scribbling would have amused Freud, but I felt I was creating more with those circles than the other campers were with their class assignment.

It was a lonely time for me. During "Team

Time," when everyone got together to talk, I waited for others to come to me. No one did. I felt awkward with people my own age because I had always interacted with the older teens who attended Teen Mania. I didn't know what to talk about with kids my age. Besides, if my fellow Christians were drawn only to the God in me, which is what I believed to be true, well, no wonder I was alone. He was missing in action.

I didn't understand. What more could I do? Surely He could see how hard I was trying. Bible Boot Camp was the last place I wanted to be, but I was there for Him. Working for Him. What did He want from me anyway? Just like at home, all of the kids at camp seemed to get along with Him just fine. I was the leper. What had I done to deserve being forsaken? Deserted? Scorned?

That's when I started getting mad.

After two weeks, I returned home to Texas, more confused than ever. My parents are such true believers — there's no bull about their faith — that I'm sure they were disappointed in me. But I felt utterly disappointed in God. I scrolled back through my memory to a time when I was nine years old. I was playing with my dolls in the doll-house I built with Papa and my sister, Charity, when I began to wonder about what happened to us after we die. I left my dolls and found Papa hanging shirts in his walk-in closet. "What happens after we die, Papa?" I asked. "Well, what happens is that we go to Heaven," he said. "How do you know?" I asked. "Have you been there?" Papa hesitated, but only for a moment. "I know because the Bible says so," he said. I needed to know more. "Why does the Bible say so?" I asked. "Because it just does," Papa said. Now, Papa could have had his mind on something else, or maybe he was in a rush to get somewhere and didn't have the time to go into such a deep discussion, I don't know. But what I took from that conversation was that it was wrong for me to ask questions, that it was bad asking such questions. I just had to have faith. Frustrated, I had meandered back to my room and resumed playing with my dolls when I thought to myself, *Is this what God does, just plays with us like little dolls? Is that why we're not allowed to ask questions?* Suddenly I felt like God was patronizing me, playing with me, that we were all just toys in His dollhouse. I didn't want it to be true.

I had forgotten about that conversation with myself years earlier. But now I thought, *Were my suspicions back then true? What else could it be?*

"God," I prayed. "Is that what is happening here? Are You taunting me? Playing with me, like I'm a little doll? Are we all just toys? Are You playing with all of us? If You're not playing a game, why can't I feel the Holy Spirit? Why do I still not have answers?"

Silence.

I began splitting into two Hannahs after that. The one I pretended to be for Papa and my mother: the faithful evangelical girl who thrived on blind faith and lived to do the work of God, as they had done for all of their lives. And then there was the girl I was secretly becoming: a lonely skeptic who was headed for a serious crisis of faith.

Papa always told us kids we didn't need to party because we had the party going on inside us, which was Jesus.

Now I wondered, *Why don't I feel the party?*

# 7
## SPEAKING IN TONGUES

Why should all believers receive and exercise the gift of tongues? . . . When we speak in tongues we are saying things in a spiritual language our enemy Satan cannot understand . . . when we pray in tongues, we are assured that we are praying as we should because the Holy Spirit is praying through us.

— JOYCE MEYER,
*FILLED WITH THE SPIRIT: UNDERSTANDING GOD GOD'S POWER IN YOUR LIFE*

When I was fifteen, I accepted an internship at the New Life Church in Colorado Springs. The internationally known megachurch was on the verge of a colossal scandal in which its founder, Ted Haggard, a family friend, would be forced to resign in disgrace after admitting to homosexual trysts and illicit drug use. The married pastor was "outed" by a paid male escort who went public with the allegations in response to Ted's vocal support for a Colorado referendum banning gay marriage. The referendum passed, but Ted was ruined, confessing to his flock of fourteen thousand members, "I am a deceiver and a liar. There's a part of my life that is so repulsive and dark that I have been warring against it for all of my adult life." We were as shocked as everyone else.

My internship took place a few months before the scandal broke, while Ted was still at the helm of the New Life Church. Papa encouraged me to accept an invitation to intern at the ministry's Desperation Leadership Academy (Desperate for Jesus). He said it was a great opportunity to continue to feed my hunger for religious knowledge. Only one hundred of the coveted internships were given, and no one turned them down. I wasn't about to be the first. I never passed up a chance to learn more about faith and religion and why people believed what they did. Not only that, I welcomed any social opportunity that Papa approved of. Growing up, I wasn't allowed to just "hang out" or spend the night at a friend's house, the way other kids were, so I never passed up a chance to be around other people.

Not surprisingly, the academy was challenging, and I found that I really enjoyed learning the skills of a leader. We interns were required to wake up at five in the morning to work out, attend classes all day, and then go to a separate worship service for us each evening. After each of those evening services, the worship leader invited anyone who wanted to receive the Holy Spirit to come forward.

I was raised to believe that, when you're good with God, you're able to speak in tongues, which is supposedly the language of the Holy Spirit, and comes out sounding like a kind of gibberish unique to each person who experiences it. The practice has roots in the Old and New Testaments and is thought to have been popularized by Pentecostal churches in the early 1900s. Saint Paul called it "speaking in the tongues of angels," and for many conservative Christians it's the penultimate earthly experience, a gift from Heaven given only to those who are imbued with the Spirit. At least in this world, it doesn't get any better than reaching the point in your walk with God where he speaks through you. In spite of my lingering doubts about evangelical doctrine, I wanted my Christianity to be real, and I thought maybe this was a way to find out where exactly I stood with God. "And when you are filled with the Holy Spirit, you speak in tongues," said Saint Paul.

So, one night, at the conclusion of the evening service, as everyone was praying and worship music was playing, I whispered to my spiritual leader that I wanted to be prayed over to speak in tongues. "I don't know that I ever really have, and I want it to be real," I admitted.

I'd heard people speak in tongues before, plenty of times. They always sounded like cackling chickens to me. I'd heard it from my own mother and from teenagers who were saved by Papa at his youth rallies. I'd even tried it a few times myself, but it never came naturally. I was pretty sure I was just pretending.

That night, after my request, everyone started laying their hands on me, on my head and my shoulders and my back and my arms. I felt overwhelmed and anxious. Was it performance anxiety that was causing my underarms to sweat and my heart to skip? What if it didn't happen? I wondered. What if the Holy Spirit really wasn't somewhere inside me, and I couldn't receive the gift of speaking in tongues? Would they all wonder if I was really saved? That would be really bad. Everyone knew I was a preacher's kid, and Papa was a popular guest preacher at the ministry's annual Desperation Conference. The last thing I wanted was whispers in the community that Hannah Luce was lost. I really, really wanted this to work.

The prayers kept coming, and I kept waiting. My hands turned clammy and shaky. If it didn't happen soon, if I didn't start blathering in an alien tongue, the people praying would become irritated with me. Maybe it was just my perception, but I thought I could feel them beginning to lose patience.

The Bible says the more you pray without ceasing, the more God will speak to you. No one prayed harder than I did. I had always been taught that prayer fixed everything. If you're feeling anxious, pray. If you're in pain, pray. If you lose your car keys, pray. Nothing is too big, or too small, to take to God. I prayed to be able to speak in tongues. "If I don't do this right, God, they're going to think I'm a Christian fake. Please. Help me out here. I need to do this right." I knew how it was supposed to go, speaking in tongues. It was supposed to go the way it did for a family I knew, who went to their pastor to tell him about their experience. The parents were terrible with money and going bankrupt, and they went to the pastor to pray over their misfortune. While there, they received a tingly feeling (evangelicals often cite the tingly feeling) and began rambling in a foreign, angelic tongue. Even though the language was unintelligible, they said, they still understood it was the Lord telling them to move to San Francisco. It didn't matter that it was irrational to uproot their kids and move to a place they knew nothing about, with no money, and no job prospects, and no place to live. It didn't have to be rational. It was God's will. He spoke. They heard. Here, all I wanted was proof that the Holy Spirit was alive in me, and it wasn't happening.

As I was praying for the words to come, I looked up and saw all of these twisted faces looking down at me, praying for the Holy Ghost to speak through me. It was frightening. One woman was particularly vocal. "Start believing you have received!" she cried. "Try! Try! You're not trying hard enough! You have to try harder!" The others followed suit and began chanting louder as well. Everyone was touching me. I had heard so many people in the past describe the process as beautiful, but for me it was just frenzy and cause for more confusion.

I remembered a devotional written by Pastor Kenneth Copeland. "Heavenly Father, I am a believer. I am Your child and You are my Father. Jesus is my Lord. I believe with all my heart that Your Word is true. Your Word says if I will ask, I will receive the Holy Spirit. So in the Name of Jesus Christ, my Lord, I am asking You to fill me to overflowing with Your precious Holy Spirit. Jesus, baptize me in the Holy Spirit. Because of Your Word, I believe that I now receive and I thank You for it. I believe the Holy Spirit is within me and, by faith, I accept it. Now, Holy Spirit, rise up within me as I praise God. I fully expect to speak with other tongues, as You give me the utterance."

Still nothing.

I was getting colder and sweatier by the minute, and I didn't like the sensation of people's hands all over me. I felt so torn as I sat there, waiting and praying. I wanted my experience to be real, for my faith, as well as for all of them to see that their good work had paid off, but I just wasn't feeling it. The Bible says, "Suddenly a sound like the blowing of a violent wind came from Heaven and filled the whole house where they were sitting. They saw what seemed to be tongues of fire that separated and came to rest on each of them. All of them were filled with the Holy Spirit and began to speak in other tongues as the Spirit enabled them." I was calling out to God to bring clarity to a moment that was unclear, but the only sounds I heard were the voices of my spiritual leader and my peers, and they all sounded as frantic as I felt.

That same summer, before I went to Colorado Springs, I asked Papa to baptize me. I had been baptized when I was four or five, but I really felt as if I needed spiritual cleansing before I went off to Ted's church. Whenever Papa baptized a kid at his events, they seemed to emerge from the water brand new. That's what I was looking for. I wanted to be cleansed of my sins, reborn in the spiritual sense. We went to a nearby lake and waded in. Papa held me as I lay back in the water, submerging myself. When I re-emerged, he had me scream, "The Devil Will Never Have Me!" I had gotten some peace from that. But now, as I tried and still couldn't conjure up the Holy Spirit, I wondered if the baptism hadn't served its purpose to cleanse me of my sins.

Why couldn't I be like everyone else I knew and just have faith without asking questions? I always had to find out for myself, and I didn't like most of the answers I was getting. What I seemed to be discovering was that I would never get the tingly feeling everyone talked about, nor was I going to start speaking in tongues. Not unless I faked it.

It seemed as if a long time passed, and I could tell that my collaborators were getting tired of encouraging me. *It's now or never,* I told myself. *If I don't play this right, they'll think I'm not saved.* I took a deep breath and prayed for the best. *Okay, I have to do it,* I said.

Closing my eyes again, I tried to block out the voices of the others, and I started chanting. I felt silly at first, but I was surprised at how easy it was. The words sounded like some unique tribal dialect. Ashunda! Badabadoshobadabada! As soon as I started, the tension that had taken over the room earlier suddenly subsided. Ashunda! Bada. Ashashunda. Babadoshabunda. The hands came off, and the voices of the others turned joyful. As I got louder and stronger, they sounded calmer and quieter.

There's a saying that the more you speak that special, holy language, the more God will speak to you and the devil will know your name, which is a good thing because it means your credentials as an apostle of Jesus are undeniable. I babbled for a few minutes longer until I felt as if I had been convincing enough and those who worked so hard to get me to this point were satisfied (and, I admit, I had hoped all through the process that the Holy Spirit would eventually take over). Finally snapping out of my trance, I made sure I awakened with a huge smile.

From everything I'd seen and read I knew that people who speak in tongues have a sense of euphoria once it's over. I'd read it and witnessed it enough to know that needed to be my last act.

"Lord God!" I shouted. "I thank You for filling me to overflowing with Your Holy Spirit! The Holy Spirit has spoken through me! Hallelujah!" The others echoed my words. They were dancing and jumping up and down. Hallelujah! Praise Jesus! In the name of the Father and the Son and the Holy Spirit!

The moment was supposed to have been the high point of my Christian life. The pinnacle. What trumped channeling God? Instead, in my failure, once again, to be acknowledged by Him, I'd been duplicitous and conniving by pretending to speak the words of the Holy Spirit. I knew what that meant.

The Book of Mark says, "verily I say unto you, All sins shall be forgiven unto the sons of men, and blasphemies wherewith soever they shall blaspheme: But he that shall blaspheme against the Holy Spirit has never forgiveness, but is in danger of eternal damnation."

I had committed the unpardonable sin.

# 8
## SAN FRANCISCO

Men never do evil so completely and cheerfully as when they do it from religious conviction.

— BLAISE PASCAL, *PENSÉES*

With Jesus still ignoring me, I made my own party for the next couple of years. I continued in secret to read books about different faiths and religious philosophies, and I began experimenting with sinful things like cigarettes, wine, and even a little bit of weed. My appearance had changed dramatically from the little girl with butterfly clips in my hair and sparkles on my arms. I called my new style hippie chic. Mom hated the look and was always quietly grousing about it: Amy Winehouse was just coming on the music scene, and I had adopted her retro look, with a big, black beehive and thick black eyeliner drawn to resemble a cat. I packed on jewelry, twenty bracelets on one arm, ten on the other, with layers of beads around my neck. Mom was always telling me my makeup was too heavy or my skirt was too short.

My vision of the world had changed as much as my look had, but I was able to hide part of me from most of the people in my world. Unbeknownst to my parents, I had decided that I didn't see any harm in some of the distractions of earth, in secular music, or spicy movies, or books that provoked thought and questions. I didn't want to judge everyone and everything based on a charismatic evangelical reading of the Bible. Although I loved reading it for the beauty of the words and the stories, I had serious doubts about the literal interpretation of it. My parents didn't know this Hannah, not at all, and I did my best to hide her by playing the role of the obedient evangelical daughter they wanted me to be.

My curiosity didn't mean I had completely lost faith in God or my religious values, because when a boy from school said he liked me, you know, *that kind of like,* I told him it wasn't me he was attracted to, but the God in me. So much for a budding teenage romance.

I also continued to keep close ties with Teen Mania. I still helped out on the Teen

Mania campus, and I loved going on mission trips to different countries and learning about different cultures. I still accompanied Papa on his annual, multi-city "Acquire the Fire" and "BattleCry" tours of the U.S. and Canada. The mission of Teen Mania is "to provoke a young generation to passionately pursue Jesus Christ and to take his life-giving message to the ends of the Earth." Papa's traveling show, which one writer accurately described as "a mix of pep rally, rock concert, and church service," was the heart of the ministry. Papa packed stadiums with thousands of people wherever he went. It was all very upbeat and positive, and even though I didn't always love the message — in fact, sometimes I shuddered at the things he preached — I loved the electric atmosphere and the Christian rock bands, especially the Newsboys and Skillet. I felt really cool being able to hang out with them backstage. What sixteen-year-old wouldn't love being at the center of all that excitement?

BattleCry 2006 in San Francisco promised to be even more electrifying than most of Papa's revivals. More than twenty-five thousand evangelical teenagers descended on the city for the weekend, twice the number that attended the events in other cities on the tour that year. I was stoked. Papa decided at the last minute that he would hold a pre-event rally on that Friday on the steps of San Francisco's City Hall. The purpose was the usual: to affirm Jesus and take a stand against what he called "the virtue terrorists" who were destroying the youth culture in America. As a footnote in a letter to his followers announcing the rally, he noted that "these are the very City Hall steps where several months ago gay marriages were celebrated for the entire world to see."

Now it's not as if Papa had ever hidden his disapproval of homosexuality. He was and is a vocal critic of gay marriage. But this was San Francisco, the city of tolerance, and the epicenter for gay pride. Looking back, it seems to me that footnote was an invitation for trouble. Papa says he was in no way courting controversy, and that he had no intention of even touching on gay marriage — that the goal was to appeal to young people to come to Christ — but I think he should have seen the handwriting on the wall.

Mom, Charity, Cameron, and I got to the rally just as it was getting underway. As we walked across the mall toward City Hall, I saw Papa standing at the top of the steps, a

103

microphone in one hand, his Bible in the other. I was proud of my father, even if I was beginning to loathe some of his extreme Christian ideals, and I knew that his heart was right. He wasn't traveling the world, churning out scripture, for his own self-gratification. He truly believed he was called by God to be a leader in the movement to rescue a generation and change the direction of an increasingly morally corrupt — and Godless — society. For him, this was a battle between good and evil — a "reverse rebellion" ordered by the Lord himself.

I could feel the excitement in the air as I approached City Hall. No one can stir a crowd of religious kids the way Papa can. He paces and stomps and waves his arms and sometimes shouts in a screechy voice that sounds like James Brown singing "I Feel Good." His flagrant passion for sharing the Gospel, for bringing people to Christ, is contagious. I have seen thousands of kids roused to their feet, and dropped to their knees, by his words. I pushed my way through the crowd. Hundreds of young people wearing red, white, and black "BattleCry" paraphernalia waited for Papa to sound the BattleCry so they could begin "setting the captives free." (Translation: showing the nonbelievers Jesus.)

It was only as I got closer to Papa that I noticed the metal barricades dividing the street, with police officers on either side. On one side of the barricade, our group, which included teens, their parents, and youth pastors, pastors and staffers waved red BattleCry flags and held up placards reading, "WE HAVE A VOICE." On the other side, pockets of boisterous counter-demonstrators held angry signs and shouted obscenities. One group carried a wooden cage with a small, deranged-looking figure inside that was supposed to resemble Papa. A sign on the cage read "Ron Luce is a Faggot." I was at once curious and fearful. This was not going to be the usual Ron Luce joyful lobby for Christ.

My father stood in the rain at the top of the City Hall steps, stoic but determined, surrounded by his loyal army of young recruits. "Are you ready to go to battle for your generation?" he shouted, his voice echoing loudly around the plaza. His followers roared, "Yes!" and waved their red flags. Papa said, "You guys are caught in the middle of a battle, and it's time that people who love God, the decent people of the land, stand up and raise their voice and say, 'You know what? We're not going to let these people steal a generation without making some noise.' "

"BattleCry!" the teenagers roared.

"BattleCry!"

The other side countered by pumping their fists and shouting ugly epithets. I could see in Papa's face that he was taken aback by their hostility. One man leading the protestors, who I later learned was a California state assemblyman, was especially hostile and said of us, "They're loud, they're obnoxious, they're disgusting, and they should get out of San Francisco." But it was their side calling names. They were calling Papa a "fascist" and a "faggot" and screaming at him to "Stop teaching hate!" and "Go back to Texas!" None of it sounded very tolerant to me, so I decided to cross the barricades and find out for myself why they hated us so much.

I slowly made my way, as subtly as I could, to the other side of the street, toward a group of men, some dressed in drag, some wearing priestlike robes, who called themselves "The Sisters of Perpetual Indulgence." The group is well known for using religious imagery to bring attention to sexual intolerance, something I didn't know at the time. Ron Luce in a cage was typical of their propaganda, and I might have thought it funny if it wasn't aimed at my dad. At the same time, I could understand that they wanted to make a point.

Papa was an outspoken critic of the "social constructs" that violated the laws of the scriptures. But his condemnation of homosexuality ("You shall not lie with a male as with a woman. It is an abomination." Leviticus 18:22) was fierce and felt more personal for me than many of his other judgments. I had gay friends by then, although most of them were deep in the closet. Their hearts were pure, and I couldn't fathom a loving God punishing such good people. Not only that, I'd witnessed the torture my evangelical peers suffered when they had homosexual thoughts or leanings. So many of them had chosen inauthentic lives because they feared that if they followed their hearts they risked the wrath of God, no less than that of their parents and the church. That seemed like a terrible injustice to me. But the protestors were so angry it was hard to feel any kind of camaraderie with them.

I tried, nevertheless. I was wearing my favorite brown jacket with a rainbow peace sign on the back, which I thought said what I stood for, but they were too busy shouting through bullhorns to notice: "Christian fascists GO AWAY. Racists. Sexists. Antigay," they chanted. As terrified as I was, I

107

decided to introduce myself to a few of the most malicious-acting protestors. "Hi, I'm Hannah," I said, purposely not mentioning my last name. I certainly didn't want them to know I was the daughter of the man they thought should be in a cage, but I really wanted to hear what they had to say. "What's going on?" I asked. "What's all this about?"

They were friendly enough at first, answering my questions with vindictive claims through polite smiles. It reminded me of a lot of hard-line Christians who impale people who have committed what they consider some affront to Jesus, yet smile beatifically while they're doing it. "Which side are you on?" one of the protestors asked. I hesitated, legitimately unsure of my answer. "Um," I said finally. "I'm not on any side. I'm just curious." *Why do there always have to be sides?* I asked myself.

I stood there for a few moments, continuing to ask questions, and then, out of the corner of my eye, I saw members of Papa's staff, wearing their BattleCry jackets and buttons, looking my way. I tried hiding my face, so they didn't recognize me, but it didn't do any good. They saw my frantic expression and headed for me, calling my name. "Hannah? Hannah!" *This can't be good,* I thought. The protestors immediately turned on me. I tried explaining that I was sympathetic to their cause, and that I was only at the rally by default. I hadn't misrepresented myself, I said. Not intentionally anyway. The protestors scoffed at me and mocked everything I said. Meanwhile, the BattleCry people stood there looking at me as if I were a traitor. As if I had betrayed them and Papa the way Peter had betrayed Jesus when he denied knowing him.

Maybe I was a traitor. But I was only sixteen. *I can't choose,* I cried to myself. *I want to love everybody. I want everyone to feel accepted. Why are you making me into a fighter?* One of the protestors pushed his sign at me, as if insisting that I display my loyalty. My eyes filled with tears. I was so conflicted. I wanted them to know I cared, but I loved Papa, too. I wished they could have known him as I did, as a kind and well-meaning man. Or were they right when they called our group "Christian fascists. Racists. Sexists. Antigay"? I grabbed the sign, which read, "The Christian Right is Wrong." I did it because I wanted the protestors to know I cared, even though it was clear from their faces that they didn't care about me. It was my way of saying, "I've come from a life of pain, too. I want you to talk with me.

I want to hear your stories and understand your pain!" But just as I did I felt nails digging into my arm. Someone was trying to pull me away.

I swung around and came face-to-face with one of Papa's beefy security guards. "Get away from those people and don't hold their signs!" he shouted. I jerked my arm away from him. "Don't touch me!" I shouted back. I looked around, first at the angry faces of the protestors, then at Papa's people. Panic shot through my body. *I have to get out of here. I have to get away,* I said to myself. I was disgusted with myself for participating in a rally that hurt people on both sides, and I was disappointed at the rage and cruelty I felt from the protestors, whom I related to more than I did to my own people. So I bolted. I ran as fast as I could. I didn't know where I was going. I just had to escape. My heart ached, and I felt utterly alone. I was swept with emotions I couldn't express and didn't understand anyway. I loved and respected Papa, but because of his harsh Christian judgments he and his ministry had become a lightning rod for anger and frustration.

I'd read a statement attributed to the Nobel Prize–winning novelist and playwright, Sinclair Lewis, who said: "When fascism comes to America, it will be wrapped in the flag and carrying a cross." Was that my father? If so, I didn't want any part of that. I needed to get away. Away from that rally. Away from Teen Mania. Away from the people I loved most in the world and the only life I knew.

But where would I go?

The only place I could go. Home. But the day I arrived back in Texas I made a deal with God. "Lord God," I prayed. "I am beginning to doubt You. I've tried and tried to get You to speak to me. I've repeatedly prayed to be able to hear Your voice. Yet You stubbornly refuse to answer my prayers. From now on, You won't be speaking through me until You can speak to me.

"Amen."

# 9
# ORU

It is not fashionable to teach college students to develop their spiritual life. Many university educations leave students virtually undeveloped in the most meaningful part of their existence. Indeed, some seriously damage what Christian convictions students may have had.

— ORAL ROBERTS, FROM HIS ADDRESS
TO THE FIRST CLASS AT ORU,
SEPTEMBER 7, 1965

I graduated high school ready to break free from my religious prison. I didn't want to go to Oral Roberts University. My parents had both gone there, and I was in the middle of a major mutiny from my fundamentalist Christian upbringing. I'd jumped the evangelical ship, at least in my heart, and I was still treading water, trying to figure out where I might rediscover some kind of faith. What I knew for sure was that

I wanted to get as far from my evangelical roots as I possibly could, and ORU is the largest charismatic Christian university in the world: certainly not the escape I was hoping for.

I had seen the world through evangelical glasses, and I wanted to revisit some of my favorite places with fresh eyes, so I suggested a couple of universities in Europe. My parents pushed for ORU, saying that it was important to them that I continue to surround myself with good Christian people. How could they gauge my religiousness if I were far away at Oxford in England or at the University of Amsterdam or Stockholm University? But ORU had offered me a free ride, a full scholarship awarded to qualified students who exemplified "a whole person lifestyle in that they are desirous of developing not just intellectually, but emotionally, spiritually, and physically." I figured the reason they wanted me there was more about Papa than me; he was on the board.

I went off to college, silently kicking and screaming. I tried focusing on the positives: ORU is a great school. It always made a good showing in college rankings, in respected publications like the *Princeton Review* and *U.S. News.* And at least it was in a city, Oklahoma's second largest, on a river.

I loved the water. I told myself there were congregations filled with good Christian girls who would kill to get into ORU. Who was I to grouse about it?

My freshman year didn't start off well.

On the first day there, all of the incoming students are required to sign an honor code pledge.

It began like this: "In signing the honor code pledge, I fully recognize that Oral Roberts University was founded to be and is committed to being a leading academic institution serving the interdenominational Body of Christ, offering a lifestyle of commitment to Jesus Christ of Nazareth as personal Savior and Lord. I further recognize that the university's ministry is that of providing a Whole Person education with a charismatic distinctive. It is therefore my personal commitment to be a person of integrity in my attitude and respect for what Oral Roberts University is in its calling to be a Christian university."

These were some of the vows I was signing off on:

To apply myself wholeheartedly to my intellectual pursuits and to use the full powers of my mind for the glory of God. (I promised myself I'd try.)

To grow in my spirit, by developing my

own relationship with God. (I'd been trying to do that for years.)

To develop my body with sound health habits by completing the required aerobics program and by participating in wholesome physical activities. (Sounded good to me.)

To cultivate good social relationships and to seek to love others as I love myself. I will not lie; I will not steal; I will not curse; I will not be a talebearer. I will not cheat or plagiarize; I will do my own academic work and will not inappropriately collaborate with other students on assignments. (I'd have to work on the cursing part.)

To at all times keep my total being under subjection from all immoral and illegal actions and communications, whether on or off campus. I will not take any illegal drugs or misuse any drugs; I will not engage in or attempt to engage in any illicit, unscriptural sexual acts, which include any homosexual activity and sexual intercourse with one who is not my spouse through traditional marriage of one man and one woman. I will not drink alcoholic beverages of any kind; I will not use tobacco; I will not engage in other behavior that is contrary to the rules and regulations listed in the Student Handbook. (Wow.)

I was always the kind of kid who sat in the

front of the class. I loved learning, and I wanted to be as close to the teacher as I could get. My first class at ORU was a Spanish class and, as always, I took a seat in front.

The teacher seemed nice enough. He was tall and gangly with chalky white skin and a seemingly mild manner. But as class got going, he stopped speaking en Español and began blabbering in tongues. His hands were shaking, his body was gyrating, and he was shouting unintelligible words. It sounded to me like the people in the movies when they were having sex.

Once that was over, he pointed to a boy in the class and said, "I believe God has a word for you." The boy resisted coming to the front of the class, but the professor insisted. "You never say never to God because He has a funny sense of humor, and He'll get you back." When the boy (reluctantly) walked up front, the teacher instructed all of us who were seated in the front two rows to pray over the kid.

This professor began every class asking who needed a prayer. We'd pray over that person, then we'd pray over the school and go in whatever direction God was leading him. *Aren't we supposed to be learning Spanish?* I asked myself. It was a rhetorical question. I already knew the answer: God trumped education, so who was he, the professor, to interrupt God's words just because he was supposed to teach a class? The professor wasn't dedicated to educating students. He was more interested in being on the front lines of the Christian battle to save them from missing their calling.

That same professor then called me into his office one afternoon. Once we got inside he started doing his shaking, grinding, groaning thing. I didn't think much of it. *God's comin', I guess,* I told myself. I sat there quietly for a while. Finally, I asked, "What's going on, Professor?" He responded, "This always happens when God's spirit starts speaking to me."

I'll admit it. I was bitter and cynical. But I was still always interested when people said God spoke to them. I was always curious about what God had to say. So I decided to wait. He started speaking in tongues. Then he switched to English and said something about how I was meant to be a prophetess for my generation. God had chosen me as a chosen one. The professor got my attention. He closed his eyes, and then they flew open again. His face was flushed red. "That one!" he cried. I was startled. "What?" I asked. His eyes widened even more. He poked his index finger toward my wrist. "That!" he shouted, pointing. "That has a spirit in it!" He was talking about a bracelet I was wearing. "It's a bad spirit! Take it off!" I explained that I had gotten the bracelet during a trip to Australia. I had worn it many times and never had a problem. "Maybe not now!" he said. "But it's an evil spirit, and it will hinder your anointing."

I was shocked; I hadn't heard stuff like that in a while. I removed the bracelet anyway. I just wanted to learn Spanish. After that I moved to the back of the class.

I tried to stay positive that first semester. I kept telling myself that you always have to take the good with the bad. But the bad just kept on coming. I knew I was partially responsible for the way things were going. I was a creative person in an advertising and marketing major, so I didn't like my classes, and I was a Christian contrarian in a Christian university that wasn't known for tolerating any kind of religious dissent.

At least I didn't think so then.

My attitude affected my whole beginning college experience, and I wasn't a good student. Some of it was my fault. But some of it was that I just didn't belong. Hardcore Christians don't take well to rebels. One professor in particular that semester was especially put off by me and my way of thinking. She taught an advertising class I was taking, and she began every session the way my Spanish professor did, by asking who in the class needed prayers then ordering a group of us to pray over each person with a request. The prayer requests ranged from, "I need prayer for a class assignment," or "I need prayer because I need to lose weight and I gorged at lunch," to "I need prayer because my father is dying" and "I need prayer for an unspoken," which meant it was something really bad that the person wasn't willing to share.

I didn't like the professor — I thought she was a poser — so when she called on me, I told her I didn't pray in public. It was just to get under her skin. Of course I prayed in public! I had just prayed with my Dad at one of his events in front of thousands of people. When I told her, respectfully, no, she walked me out of the classroom and insisted on knowing why I was defying her. I said, "I just don't feel comfortable doing that." She looked at me with disgust, but what could she do?

The next time we had class, she announced that things were going to change a little. She said rather than asking everyone to "pray in public" (and she emphasized the phrase), we were to turn to our neighbor and pray. I was seventeen years old and trying to be the best Christian I could, but I was still going through the despair of my predicament with God, and this woman was trying to force me to pray. She watched as I turned to my neighbor, a nice girl named Mary. "What do you need prayer over?" I asked my classmate. She named a couple of things, and I told her I'd prayer for her privately, on my own time.

The professor came over to Mary and asked about me, as if I wasn't even there. "Is she giving you a hard time?" Poor Mary. She was caught in between. "Oh, no," she said timidly. "Has she prayed over you?" Mary fidgeted for a minute. The teacher put her hands on her hips. "Well?" she asked. "No," Mary said, sighing. "She doesn't feel comfortable praying in class."

I should have just dropped the class, but I didn't want to give her the satisfaction of giving me an F. After that I was dead to her — until it came to our final presentation, which would result in a make-or-break grade.

Each of us had to come up with a theme for an advertising campaign. Mine was, "Treasure Island: Where Your Dreams Come True." Knowing the odds were against me, I put everything I had into that project. I painted my own poster with a colorful scene of a mysterious but beautiful place I called Treasure Island. I wrote a pitch to go with it. My idea was to sell this elusive place. One of the criteria of the project was that we had to include a contact number. At the bottom of the poster I wrote: "For more information, call 1-800-PSYCHIC." I thought it was clever. From the ad, you didn't really know what you'd be getting into if you traveled to Treasure Island, but call the number and you'd find out which of your dreams could come true.

The class loved it. But when the poster was handed back, I turned it over and saw a big, red D. I went to the teacher and asked why. She stammered and said that she would have given me an A except for the 1-800-PSYCHIC reference. Everyone knew that psychics practiced black magic, she said, and that went against the university's honor code.

I was livid. "This isn't fair," I said. "I did everything right. You were just looking for something to catch me on." I was surprised, but she took pity on me. She said if I removed the number from my poster, she'd change my grade to a C. I needed the passing grade more than the pride of upholding my principles, so I did, and she did.

At the end of the semester I sought her out and apologized for being disrespectful at the beginning of the school year. "I'm truly sorry," I said. "I was out of line and I'd like to take you to coffee to make up for it." She took me up on the offer. We went to a coffee house in town and, over lattes, she told me that I'd reminded her of herself when she was young. "I see a lot of me in you," she said. I thought that was going overboard. Then she said, "I sense there's an anointing on you, and you're choosing to ignore it." I took a breath and waited for her to lay her hands over me and start speaking in tongues, but she didn't.

She finished her latte and picked up the tab, and we left.

That teacher embodied everything I expected to dislike about my college experience. She had expectations of me because of who I was and where we were. But I just wanted to be me.

# 10
## FITTING IN

Well, I can't figure out God.
> — ORAL ROBERTS, IN AN
> INTERVIEW WITH LARRY KING

I almost failed my first semester, so after that I switched my major from advertising and marketing to theological historical studies. My main reason for doing it was that I was hoping to gain insight into why I was the way I was. And, deep, deep down I was still harboring the tiniest bit of hope that I'd come to better understand the Christian faith of my family. The other reason is that I was more artsy than business-minded, and if I never had to take another accounting or advertising class I'd be a happy camper. Strike that. I'd be a *happier* camper. Meaning that I'd be less miserable.

Honestly, I didn't have high hopes for my new major. More religion? Sometimes I wondered if I had a sadistic streak. At least with business courses I'd only have to crunch numbers and give presentations about fake places and products. Now I'd have to study the same books and listen to the same stuff that had been crammed down my throat my whole life. "Oh, stop your complaining, Hannah," I told myself. I did, and I prayed for the best.

It was my first day in my Christian Ethics class. Dr. Chris Green was our professor. He was young and handsome, with kind of spiky blond hair, and he dressed more like us than the other professors. He introduced himself and said, "Before we start," then asked those of us with evangelical backgrounds to raise our hands. Of course, almost everyone did. Then he said the life-changing words I will never forget. He said that for most of us, everything we'd been taught about Christianity thus far was wrong. I waited for the punch line. "In this class, we will tear down your Christian foundation, and you'll feel homeless for a while," he said. "But if you stick with it, your faith will be rebuilt on a foundation of what Christianity is really meant to be."

I burst into tears.

For most of my life, for as long as I had been able to think for myself, every time I asked questions about Christianity, I was told either that I was being rebellious or that I was flat-out wrong. With that one introduction Dr. Green had given me the gift of redemption from my Christian guilt. What I drew from his words was that everything I had been taught my whole life about God and His expectations of me might not be completely right, and maybe I had some legitimate questions, and maybe I still had a chance to get some of the answers I had been seeking for a lifetime. Maybe it was Dr. Green's voice, and not necessarily God's voice, that could help me find my faith. I couldn't wait to get started.

I was the only girl in my theological history major, and most of us were seditious pastors' kids. We were a class of only fifty or so students, and a lot of the other students on campus ostracized us. I think they were perplexed by us, really. They didn't understand why we were studying things like Islam and Hindu customs and probing the origins of the charismatic arm of Christianity and its relevance in contemporary society. Occasionally one of us was approached by one of the more radical charismatic Christian students objecting to our presence on campus, but that didn't happen too often, and when it did, we calmly held our own because our classes had primed us for good debates.

My classmates in my major affirmed my feelings of isolation from the church. I saw myself in them, and they saw themselves in me, and we saw ourselves as the "free thinkers" in a culture of closed minds. I loved what I was learning. Our studies called for us to question and challenge religious dogma, and our professors provoked our thoughts. I took classes like Divine Healing, Christian Apologetics, Charismatic Theory, and The History of Christianity. One of my favorite courses was all about the major religions of the world.

In my Charismatic Theology class, we dissected the origins of indoctrinated symbols such as healing the sick, raising the dead, and demonic powers. The professor didn't insist that the charismatic Christian interpretation of those things was necessarily correct. He assigned books, some of the same ones that Papa had taken away from me years earlier, and he encouraged us to question the core beliefs of our parents' religion and support our own conclusions. It was okay to ask questions, my professor said, and he affirmed that critical thinking was healthy. Without questions, you remain blocked at the beginning of your spiritual journey. (I had always felt that blind belief in the literal interpretation of the scriptures was limiting and stood in the way of my walk with God, and here he was, validating that.)

I began spending all of my time with my church history friends. I started what I called "Cultural Nights" for our group at which, every week, we'd gather together and share ideas about all sorts of provocative things. One night the topic might be books or art; the next time, we'd be discussing world politics, racial issues, or Christian ethical dilemmas. We'd carry a cooler of Pabst Blue Ribbon down to the river, where we'd start a bonfire and talk into the wee hours of the morning. I could hardly believe that I could find that kind of freedom and independence at ORU.

*This must be heaven,* I said, chuckling to myself.

For me, it really was.

For the first time in my life, I felt as though I belonged. I wasn't an alien in my own skin anymore. I began to feel comfortable getting to know myself and being myself, and I worked at not judging others and myself so harshly. I started to see that there was room for us and them in religion, whatever faith it was. By studying the history of evangelical faith and how it came to be, I began to understand that a lot of my father's rhetoric came from what he had been taught, not from God Himself, and I started to let go of my paranoia about what I had always perceived as God's rejection of me. I could finally stop watching for some extraterrestrial to come out of the trees to speak to me. I could stop looking for signs that God existed.

Papa had come to his own conclusions about God and the church, and I was forming my own. We didn't have to agree. However it all shook out I would respect Papa's beliefs, and I hoped that he would respect me for searching so long and hard to find mine. I realized that whatever the future brought, I didn't have to focus on our differences. What I knew to be true was that Papa was a man of tremendous integrity. He truly cared about people, and his faith was genuine. I could support that.

Papa came to ORU to appear during the biannual campus Christian revival. My militant church history classmates had started a Twitter account they called #Twapel for tweets about chapel. People posted anonymously, so the comments could get pretty mean. All of our guest speakers were critiqued, and no one was spared. I remember this charismatic Christian evangelist couple who came to speak, and comments flew about her big helmet hair and his man boobs. The site became really big on campus, and students began sitting in chapel, secretly tweeting all during services. I tweeted myself occasionally and got a kick out of other people's tweets. Until the criticisms turned to my Papa. Then it wasn't funny anymore.

It happened during the night service on the first day of the fall revival week. Everyone on campus was required to attend chapel that night. Papa was the featured preacher. As I sat there watching him do his thing, I checked the Twapel site and saw the tweets were flying. "Whack job speaking," one person wrote. "Boring!" someone else tweeted. On one hand, I agreed with some of the things people were saying. Papa was spewing his usual fundamentalist Christian rhetoric, and I opposed a lot of it. On the other hand, I loved my father and felt the need to defend him, even if it was to my church history buddies.

I was really torn and didn't know what to do. I walked out of the service in tears that first night, but I was still facing a week's worth of revival services, and Papa would be speaking at a lot of them. I couldn't bear the idea of having to sit in chapel, knowing what the kids were tweeting. When I asked them if they could just go easy on Papa — because he was my father — they said they didn't understand. Everyone was fair game. Why should Papa get special treatment? I felt betrayed.

Desperate, I went to Dr. Green and explained my dilemma. He always had answers, and he comforted me and assured me that everything would work out. The next morning in charismatic theology class, he confronted our group. "I don't know who is playing into all this," he said, "but I'm sure you know who you are." His wisdom inspired me. "It's okay to analyze things," he said. "It's not okay to criticize someone for their beliefs." The tweets stopped after that. Another lesson learned.

# 11
## MEETING AUSTIN

We were very different, and we disagreed
about a lot of things, but he was always
so interesting, you know?

— JOHN GREEN,
*THE FAULT IN OUR STARS*

It was the beginning of my last year at ORU
when I started hearing about this incredible
new guy on campus. I had taken on the role
of a sort of chaplain on my dorm room floor
the year before, and all of the younger girls
came to me for counsel, which usually
involved either talking about boys or solving
a crisis of faith of some kind. I was a good
listener and pretty levelheaded, and I
thought it was sweet that the younger girls
thought I had the answers they needed.
Whenever they came knocking at my door,
burdened with a problem, or just wanting
to chatter about this and that, I'd make tea
and we'd sit by the space heater in my dorm

room, talking until the tea was gone or the problem was solved.

One day, just after the fall semester began, a couple of the girls, one a freshman, the other a sophomore, came to me wanting to discuss the kinds of qualities they thought they should be looking for in a husband. The girls said they were bored with their lives. The only thing worth thinking about was that one day in the not too distant future they would be planning elaborate weddings with all of the trimmings and shopping for frilly white bridal gowns. They were typical ORU girls in that they were there as much, and probably more, for the opportunity to find good Christian husbands than to study or prepare for careers. One of them said her parents told her if she couldn't find a husband meeting all of her requirements at ORU, she wouldn't find one anywhere. That didn't surprise me. It's what all good evangelical parents wanted for their daughters: a nice, clean-cut evangelical boy.

For me, listening to the girls talk was almost like listening to a foreign language. I just didn't understand someone who was eighteen or nineteen wanting so much to be married when there were so many other interesting things to do, like traveling and meeting people and changing the world. But listen I did as they described what they considered to be perfect husband material. This hot new guy that was walking around campus was it.

It turned out to be Austin.

Austin Anderson was new to the university. He had come there straight from serving two tours in Iraq, and he was creating quite a stir. He was a little bit older than most of the rest of us, twenty-five at the time. He was tall and strapping, with a smile to die for, and he had that rare presence that made him a magnet for girls, who wanted to date him, and boys, who wanted to be him.

That day in my dorm room was the first time I'd ever heard of him. "This new guy named Austin" was all the two girls could talk about. How cute he was. What a kidder he was. He was a Marine. He drove a big, black pickup truck and rode a motorcycle. On and on. I humored them and pretended to be interested but, honestly, I was barely paying attention. I was much more interested in discussing the kinds of things I talked about with my small group of church history classmates. Besides, I was dating someone at the time and wasn't looking for a boyfriend for myself. And even if I had been looking, this guy didn't fit the description of what I found appealing in a boy. I liked the intellectual types, the ones who always had their head in big, brainy books.

I didn't have a lot of friends at ORU besides my church history friends, and that was by design, but I think the younger girls felt kind of protective of me. They didn't know that I had a life outside of school and that, in my spare time, I really enjoyed being by myself and poking around the city, doing things like talking to homeless people about their stories, or rummaging through the books on the dollar table at the occult bookshop, or grabbing a smoke with a stranger at the Star Avenue Hookah Lounge. The girls who told me about Austin were always trying to get me to socialize more with their friends on campus, and they constantly invited me to join them in whatever they were doing.

That day, they asked if I'd join them for lunch in the cafeteria the following afternoon. "C'mon, Hannah! So you can meet everyone!" they said. I agreed, reluctantly. I knew they wanted to show off their "older" friend. "What can it hurt?" I said. "I'll see you tomorrow."

I almost didn't go. Spending my time with a bunch of giggling teenaged girls, talking about boys, which was bound to be the topic of conversation, wasn't my idea of a productive afternoon. But that morning I had been assigned to write some pretty heavy stuff for one of my theology classes, and I'd decided I needed a break. So I walked over to the dining hall to meet my young friends.

I was irritated almost from the moment I got there. I met the girls, we got our lunches, and I followed them with my tray to a table where a bunch of students I didn't recognize were talking and joking around. All of them were girls except for the boy they were fussing over. He wore a golf shirt and ball cap over his razor cut. When I tell you he was huge, I mean he was so tall and muscular that his frame literally took up a chair and a half. And he had a big voice to match. He didn't talk. He bellowed. And he oozed charisma and energy. I didn't know who he was, nor did I care. I thought he was arrogant, and I instantly disliked him.

I purposely sat on the edge of the group, rather than with the group, and picked at my lunch, paying little attention to Mr. Popularity, because he was getting plenty from everyone else. Those girls were drooling over him. I'm sure he was trying to catch my eye just because I was ignoring him. I

135

could tell he was used to being the center of attention, and there was no way I was going to make a contribution to his already inflated ego. I was about half finished with my salad when one of the girls turned to me, all giddy and excited, and said, "What do you think?" "Of what?" I asked. "Of him?" she responded, tipping her head toward the boy. "What do you think of Austin? Isn't he hot?" So this was our evangelical heartthrob. I should have known. I just smiled. I didn't want to be associated with a group of girls who were smitten with this bigheaded, oversized jock, so I quickly wrapped up the rest of my lunch and left, walking back to my room to study for a class I had early the following morning.

Later that day, I was rushing from my dorm to my car in the parking lot, with my arms overloaded with books, late for my job at a local coffee house, when I heard someone shouting my name. "Hannah! Hey, Hannah!" I turned quickly, and the books spilled out of my arms. A boy was walking quickly toward me. *What does he want?* I wondered, annoyed with the intrusion. I couldn't place the face at first. "Hey," I said, looking up as he bent down to help me pick up my books. I'm sure I couldn't have sounded less enthusiastic. Then it registered who he was. "Oh, you're the one who was at the table today, the ones my dorm mates were talking to."

When I say that boy was grinning ear to ear, that is not an exaggeration. His teeth were dazzling white, and his eyes literally sparkled, like glitter. I didn't understand why he was so intent on talking to me. *I know your kind,* I thought. "Yeah!" he said. "I'm Austin. Austin Anderson. So, I've wanted to meet you for a while." If it wouldn't have been so rude, I would have rolled my eyes. He'd wanted to meet me for a while? I'd never seen him before a few hours ago. "Why?" I asked. Austin seemed unfazed by my lack of interest and proceeded to tell me a story about how he'd seen me a few times in chapel, sitting in the back with my headphones on, reading one of my theology textbooks.

"Yeah, I've seen you there several times," he said. "The last time you were sleeping." Now he had my attention. "I was sleeping?" I asked. "I'm sorry, but I don't remember that," I replied, but I knew he was telling the truth because I was guilty of nodding off in chapel sometimes, usually after pulling all-nighters before tests. I just thought I'd been really good at covering it up. "Oh, yeah!" he said. "It was you all right. There you were, with your head back, sleeping on the chair in chapel. I thought it was pretty cool."

I pulled my car keys out of my bag, hoping he'd take the hint, but he kept talking. "I hate this place," he said. "All of the girls around here are Daddy's girls. They don't work for anything. Them and their expensive handbags. And they all drive yellow Mustangs. All they want to do is get married." Boy, he was blunt. He sounded like me.

I was late for work. "Right now really isn't a good time," I said finally. "I've really got to go. It was nice talking to you." I turned to unlock my car door, my books heavy in my arms. "Wait," he said. "Just for a minute. Please." I was really getting annoyed. I was certain my boss at the coffee bar was getting angrier each moment that I still wasn't there. "Listen," he said. "I just got back from Iraq. Just got back! And this place is crazy! It's nothing like I thought it would be.

"Could we hang out sometime?" he asked.

Despite my efforts to dislike Austin, there was something about him that was different from the lugheads I'd compared him to and prejudged him to be. It was something I couldn't quite put my finger on. He was a bit full of himself, but in a sweet kind of way, and he was sort of rude, but he had this vulnerability about him that surprised me and that I liked.

I could tell he just needed to talk. That he wanted to get some things off his chest. "What do you say?" he asked. "Oh, I don't know," I said, wondering how the boy I was dating would take to the idea of my spending time with the campus hunk. "No, really, Hannah," he said. "I'd really like that."

I put my book on the hood of my car, grabbed a pen and paper from my (second-hand) purse, and scribbled down my number. "Here," I said, pushing the paper at him. "But I'm warning you. I'm really, really busy." He nodded and smiled, and I jumped in my car and drove off.

And I was right about my boss. When I got to the coffee house, he was behind the bar, steaming milk and steaming mad.

# 12
# BEST FRIENDS

Some people go to priests; others to poetry; I to my friends.

— VIRGINIA WOOLF, *THE WAVES*

I didn't give Austin another thought until he texted me a few days later. "Want to hang out?" he asked. My body tensed up when I read it. He seemed nice enough, but I really didn't need another friend, and I had too much work to be "hanging out." What does this guy want with me? Whatever it is, I'm not interested, but I don't want to be rude, and I'm sure I'll be seeing him around campus. "Sure," I texted back.

We drove to a park along the river and sat in my car. We settled in, and I lit a cigarette, and he pulled out a cigar. I burned incense from India, and he began talking about his workouts (he worked out twice a day) and poking fun at my freak folk music by the girl band CocoRosie. I turned down the music. "So what's your story?" I asked.

Austin was all country boy. He came from a small town in Oklahoma that was less than a square mile and had 425 people living there. He told me his father was a preacher with his own church but had died tragically in a car crash when Austin was fourteen. His mom was so frail and grief stricken that he had to arrange the funeral. After that, he played both brother and father to his younger brother and sister, he said.

His grandpa was his role model, and even though he was extremely close to his grandparents and spent a lot of time tending to the cattle and fixing fences on their ranch, he was bitter about not having had his father around for very long. He had missed a lot as a teenager because of all the responsibility he had, and he resented that. When he was a junior in high school, he decided there was more to life than anything his small town had to offer. He wanted to do something bigger and more significant with his life than he could do living there. When a Marine recruiter came to town, looking for volunteers, he saw an out and signed up.

I was surprised at how open Austin was being. He seemed really comfortable with me, and that made me feel at ease. The more he told me, the more I wanted to hear, and the more he talked. The words spilled out of his mouth like water from a breached dam. Austin said he found a lot of satisfaction in being a Marine. I got the feeling he liked bossing people around. He had served for seven years and had risen to the rank of sergeant before being honorably discharged.

"You just came out of the Marines," I said. "It can't be easy for you to be here."

Austin got mad. He said he'd dreamed of coming to ORU since his father brought him to the campus with their church when he was a little kid, but he was in Iraq when he made the decision to apply. He had prayed over it, telling God, "If this is what I think it is, I need it, Lord."

War had done a job on Austin. He told me he had nightmares a lot. "You wouldn't like them," he said, spitting the tip of his cigar out the car window. "They're all filled with blood and people dying." He said he often woke up thinking he'd killed someone, although he never did. On the day after the nightmares, he always had a hard time functioning. Sometimes he didn't sleep for days for fear he would awaken to those gruesome images. The terrible things he saw in war had made him less spiritual, less Christian, Austin said.

He didn't like the man the soldier had become, partying all the time and using girls for sex. His answer was to find someplace where he could surround himself with good, honest Christian people, and that's how he'd landed on campus. He came straight from debriefing after his last tour, with great expectations. "But I hate it here, Hannah," he said. "The people aren't what I thought they'd be. I thought they'd help me to get my faith back, but everyone seems so fake."

Austin was getting fidgety and jumpy, and his anger simmered just below the surface. I realized he was going through some serious culture shock, and he was suffering from post-traumatic stress. He was on a rant. "So how does a girl like you tolerate ORU?" he asked. "You're not the typical girl you find here." He said, "All I see here are girls driving the Mustangs their daddies bought them. That's not the kind of person I thought I'd find here. People here don't have to work for anything. They're all spoiled. I've been working since I was fourteen. I worked my butt off at war. I have three cars, and I worked for all of them. I have my own apartment. I left a small town and took a risk coming here. But I'm really disappointed in what I see so far. The people here are spoiled. They don't really care about their faith. All they care about is the material things they have and finding a husband. This isn't what I thought it would be."

Before we parted ways that night, Austin asked me about God. I knew he was questioning, but his faith was still strong, and I admired him for that. I told him I'd been bitter about religion at the university when I first got there, mostly because of the way I'd grown up, but I didn't feel that way anymore. I'd learned a lot at ORU, and I'd found some of the best teachers of my life. Because of them, I'd discovered my calling as a religious history buff and I'd settled into a comfortable life there.

I turned the subject to his impression of the people there. I was encouraging, but blunt. "Austin," I said. "I understand where you're coming from. Please believe me. I really do. I don't spend time with many people from ORU either, because I've secluded myself with my studies. It's totally fine to have opinions of people. But one thing I've learned is that you have to learn to let people surprise you." Austin nodded but said nothing. I figured, in one ear, out the other. Typical country boy.

"I have a challenge for you, Austin," I said. "Why not let people at ORU surprise you

144

for a week, and next time we talk, we'll see what you observed?" He nodded. "Okay, Hannah," he said. But I didn't have high hopes that he'd take me up on it.

When I dropped Austin off at his apartment, I surprised myself by thinking about how much I liked spending time with him. We didn't have a romantic chemistry, but I really liked him, and his presence was comforting, even when he was angry. I knew he felt the same about me. I could tell he valued my thinking. Every time I said something he hung on my words. Watching him walk into his house, I realized that I was looking forward to the next time we talked.

Austin called the next week. "Want to hang out?"

"Sure," I said.

"The park?"

"The park!" I replied.

We met there after class. The sun was shining, and I spread a blanket out on the grass, just beneath the Forty-first Street Bridge. He pulled two cigars from his pocket and lit them. One for him. One for me. He puffed on his cigar and looked at me with this bemused expression. I couldn't figure out whether he was getting ready to ask me a question or to laugh.

"What?" I asked. "What's so funny?"

"I did it," he said, breaking into a huge grin. "I did, Hannah. I did what you told me to do?"

"What did you do?" I asked.

He grinned even wider. "All week I tried to let people surprise me."

I couldn't believe it. He had really been listening. He really heard what I said. I whooped. "What?" I asked. "You really did?"

He nodded. "Ye-ah, I did."

"Wow." I said. "I'm so impressed! So? Did people surprise you?" I asked.

"You know what?" he asked, laughing now. "You know what, Hannah? I'll be damned. Some of them really did."

# 13
## MEETING GARRETT

The power of a glance has been so much abused in love stories, that it has come to be disbelieved in. Few people dare now to say that two beings have fallen in love because they have looked at each other. Yet it is in this way that love begins, and in this way only.
— VICTOR HUGO, *LES MISÉRABLES*

Austin said he owed me lunch. He wanted to do something nice for me because I had driven him to some event when his pickup was in the shop. "You pick the place," he said.

He was talking on his cell phone when he arrived at my dorm. After a couple of minutes, he finished his conversation, said good-bye to the person he was talking to, and snapped his phone shut. "We're going to the Rib Crib," he said. *Whatever happened to me picking the place?* I wondered.

"And there's a friend of mine I want you to meet," he said. "He's meeting us there."

"Huh? What friend?" I asked.

Austin grinned. "He's a professor at ORU, he loves your dad, and he's been dying to meet you."

"Oooh nooo," I said, shaking my head from side to side, vigorously.

I'd had more than my share of Teen Mania hangers-on who befriended me with the sole purpose of getting closer to Papa. I didn't need another someone with a Ron Luce obsession. I'd spent my life dealing with those people, and, at ORU, where there were lots of Teen Mania alumni, I was always shutting them down.

It's a strange feeling, having people want to cozy up to you because of who your father is. And a lot of the fundamentalist Christian kids were a little bit bizarre. I actually had more than one boy introduce himself to me out of the blue and tell me he believed God had called me to be his wife. My sister and I were always getting boys asking to "court us." That was right out of a book that all good young Christians read called *I Kissed Dating Goodbye*. It's written by a Christian guy who sells the fundamentalist concept of courting (God's way) as in Victorian times, where girls are never alone with boys, especially at night, and you save your first kiss for marriage. Dating is for everyone else (the world's way). The book's sold like crazy over the years.

I was raised on the Christian courting model. You didn't date a bunch of boys to figure out what you liked and what you didn't. You courted one boy whom you thought you'd like to marry. I played along all through high school. But I finally put my foot down when I got my first boyfriend in college and Papa not only expected him to ask permission to spend time with me, but he also had his minions at Teen Mania vet him for marriage by asking him about his sexual past.

I'm always for people supporting Papa's ministry, but I was trying to form my own identity, and here Austin was forcing it on me by inviting this guy — another Ron Luce "Maniac" — to have lunch with us. "Austin, seriously, I don't want to meet another Teen Mania person!" I said.

Austin continued to drive in the direction of the Rib Crib. He obviously thought he knew what was best for me better than I did. I sat and stared straight ahead, watching the Rib Crib sign get closer and closer. What was I going to do? Jump out of the pickup?

"You owe me for this," I said through clenched teeth as we walked into the restaurant.

A nice-looking guy was standing in the vestibule, waiting for us. He wasn't what I was expecting. Not even close. My first impression was "Oh, wow. He's a clone of Austin, only smaller." He was dressed in a golf shirt and khakis, hair cropped short, and he obviously worked out more than the average guy. I called the look Christian clean-cut. Not at all my type — I liked the brooding poet with dirty hair and skinny arms — but not bad.

"Hannah, this is Garrett. Garrett, this is Hannah," Austin said.

We walked to a table, and I whispered to Austin, "I don't want this guy to pester me with questions about Teen Mania or my dad. I'm over that." Austin seemed amused.

The first thing Garrett did was order us all beers. I worried that someone from the university would walk in and see him having a beer with a couple of students and get him fired. He certainly wasn't a typical professor.

He told me how he was teaching there part-time while studying for his doctorate in business administration. He'd spent two semesters abroad, one at the University of

150

Lima in Peru and the other in Mexico at the University of Colima. He loved teaching business courses but thought that one day he'd like to have his own company to satisfy an entrepreneurial itch. Like me, Garrett had a passion for traveling, and he'd been all over the world, mostly on mission trips, places like Russia and Panama and Chili and Belize and Guatemala. His pet project was an orphanage in Peru that he'd helped to finance.

Garrett was easy to be around. He was very cheerful and fidgety, as if he had so much to say but not enough time to say it. And rather than pepper me with questions about Papa, he shared his own experiences with the ministry.

I was surprised to hear that he had spent quite a bit of time at Teen Mania, first as a young boy, then on numerous mission trips, usually as a team leader, and most recently on a project that Papa had commissioned from ORU for a new business model for Teen Mania. I was amazed that I'd not come across him or even heard his name.

He told me a story about how, just a year earlier, he had volunteered as a team leader on a mission trip to somewhere. One of the other team leaders heard him talking with some of the kids about the Mormon religion, which he was fascinated with. She had met him on other mission trips and wasn't very friendly toward him. When she'd heard him discussing Mormonism, she reported to the person in charge that he was trying to convert the kids into Mormons. We had a good laugh over that.

After that, he said, the person in charge confronted him, someone on Papa's team I was familiar with. She wasn't my favorite person (which he was happy to hear). First she berated him about trying to convert the kids, which he denied. She asked if he was an ORU student, because he was wearing a sweater with an ORU insignia. He said, "No, I'm actually a professor there." Then she said, "I understand you own a red Hummer." Garrett answered "Yes," wondering where the conversation was headed. "You're bragging," she told him. "First about being a professor and also about owning a red Hummer. You need to be more humble."

"Then what happened?" I asked.

"You won't believe this," he said, "but she assigned me to write a paper on humility."

"You didn't do it?" I sputtered, a little too loudly, because people at the nearby tables turned to look at us.

"I did," he said sheepishly. "She kicked

me out of the program anyway."

We howled.

I didn't tell Austin this — I didn't want to give him the satisfaction — but on the way back from lunch I thought, "I really enjoy this guy. I hope we can be friends." And I thought I saw a glimmer in his eye, the kind that meant he might want to hang out with me, too.

# 14
## FRIENDSHIP GROWS

And we should consider every day lost on which we have not danced at least once. And we should call every truth false which was not accompanied by at least one laugh.

— FRIEDRICH NIETZSCHE,
*THUS SPOKE ZARATHUSTRA*

After our meeting at the Rib Crib, Garrett came with Austin a few times to my cultural nights under the Forty-first Street Bridge. He was always adding something stimulating to the conversation, usually something related to business or politics, his interests, different things from what we usually discussed. My church history friends, who were very discerning, as well as protective of our little intellectual club, welcomed him in. He was whip smart and really funny, and he added something special to the mix. I loved it when he showed up.

I was surprised when one day Garrett messaged me that he was having friends over for movie night and wanted to include me. Austin was the only person we had in common, and I figured his other friends were probably older professor types. "Why don't you come?" he asked. "Okay, cool," I said. He told me that Austin was coming and bringing his date, a girl Austin had recently told me about, but I'd yet to meet. That calmed me down a bit, to know Austin would be there and I'd know someone. Later, when I mentioned it to Austin, he perked right up and said that, yup, he'd be there with his new girl in tow. Garrett's movie nights were fun, he said.

I drove across town to Garrett's place, arriving fashionably late. I was a little bit nervous about not knowing who would be there, but I was excited to meet Austin's date. Her name was Elizabeth, and he'd told me he met her at school, although I didn't know her. She was a few years younger than he was, and what he really liked was that she didn't take any of his guff. I figured she had to be really special to get any kind of a commitment from Austin, and I knew that since he'd met her he'd given up all of his fans to be with her and wasn't even going out to bars anymore. If Austin liked her I was sure I would like her, too.

I arrived at Garrett's address and was surprised not to see Austin's pickup parked in the driveway, because Austin was always early. But the only car in the driveway besides mine was Garrett's red Hummer. Strange, I thought. I was late. Could I be the first one here? I rang the doorbell and waited. It sounded really quiet inside. I wondered if I had the time wrong. What if it wasn't the right night? How embarrassing that would be. The door swung open, and Garrett stood there with a big grin. He invited me in, and I saw I was the only one there. I looked around and noticed the lights were dim and there were candles and wine on the table, but no TV on. "Where's everyone?" I asked.

"They all canceled," Garrett said.

I thought that was odd, but I couldn't turn around and leave. I felt really uncomfortable. Why would everyone cancel? Austin said he'd be there with his girlfriend. It would be just like him to set me up. I'm going to kill him when I see him, I thought. What was I going to talk about with Garrett? He was a professor and I was a student. I felt like I was out of my league. He was as happy as a clam. He poured us each a glass of wine, and we sat on his couch and watched a movie about Mormonism. He was fascinated by their traditions. When the movie was over, we started talking. Garrett told me more about his Teen Mania experiences, and said his entire family followed the ministry and my dad whenever one of his events was nearby. I said I was surprised I'd never seen him on any of the mission trips, because he'd been on quite a few. When I finally looked at the clock to leave, it was after midnight. I'd been there for hours.

My jitters had been for naught. It had been a great night — even though I realized I'd been "had" by Austin and Garrett — and I felt our friendship took a giant leap forward. I was kind of glad it happened the way it did and it was just the two of us. When he walked me to my car I thought, "Maybe he isn't my type, but he's easy to be around." He said goodnight and promised to be in touch.

We became really close friends after that night, even closer than Austin and me, but in a different way. We took lots of walks in the park and had endless discussions about art and business and religion and government, and our beloved friend, Austin. Austin was spending most of his free time with Elizabeth. He told us he'd fallen head over heels in love with her.

Meanwhile, Garrett and I were spending more time together, too. Often it was just the two of us. I realized our relationship was peculiar in some ways. I called it unorthodox. We weren't strictly platonic friends because at times we cuddled and kissed, but we never discussed our relationship, and both of us dated other people. I saw the way he looked at me, with a glint in his eyes and a hint of a cheeky grin, a look that said he was enthralled by me, maybe even adored me, but he never said anything, and rather than complicate things by asking questions, I was happy to enjoy the friendship and see where it went.

Apparently, he revealed his feelings for me to Austin, because, every time I talked to Austin, he stirred the pot, telling me that Garrett was crazy about me and that if I gave him any sign at all that I wanted more from our relationship, he'd be all over it. "Oh, Austin!" I'd say. "Will you just stop your matchmaking? You're not very good at it anyway." And he'd respond, "I'm telling you, Hannah. That guy worships the ground you walk on." I'd answer, hoping to douse the flame he was fanning, "No, Austin, he worships my father." And Austin would conclude, "I'm telling you, Hannah. That

158

guy's falling in love with you."

I liked hearing it.

As much as Garrett and I enjoyed each other's company, as time went on I realized how different we were in some ways. He was staunch Republican and, even though I wasn't political, I was liberal in my thinking. His style fit in the classroom and on the golf course. Mine was a little bit Goth and a lot gypsy hippie. He didn't smoke, and I did. He drank an occasional beer. I liked good wine. He was secure in his conservative Christian faith, which I envied.

But our differences seemed to draw us even closer than our commonalities.

We couldn't seem to get enough of each other, and we were always challenging each other on subjects like American politics, the importance of the arts (overrated, he said), psychology (I went to therapy, he called it a waste of time), and philosophy (he once said Nietzsche was naïve), but we always ended up wanting more of each other's time.

I grew up in a household, and in a religion, in which arguments were frowned upon. In the Bible, 2 Timothy 2:22–23 says, "Have nothing to do with foolish, ignorant controversies; you know that they breed quarrels. And the Lord's servant must not be quarrelsome but kind to everyone, able to teach, patiently enduring evil, correcting his opponents with gentleness." Garrett and I called our arguments debates. I was curious about what drove him in life. He was so ambitious. He was sometimes critical of what he saw as my lack of drive. He'd say I'd rather think than do. But he had a warm heart and a compassionate spirit, and I felt safe with him. What we had in common — and it was an ironclad bond — was our thirst for something more than where we came from. Our eyes were bigger than the possibilities of our futures. We wanted the world.

There was also a playful side to our friendship. Garrett loved playing the macho guy. He wanted everyone to know he was all man. He loved talking about football and all kinds of sports stuff, and he bragged about spear fishing in Oklahoma, and hunting caribou in the Arctic Circle and monkeys in the jungles of Peru.

I suspected there was a feminine side hiding in his manly body. So one day when we were together in the park I brought along a copy of the BEM test, a test that measures androgyny, or just how male or female you are in your thoughts and feelings. The way the test works is it asks a series of questions resulting in a score from "ultra masculine" to "ultra feminine." A score that falls in the middle means you have the well-developed psyche of an androgynous mind. I never thought he'd take the bait, but he did; he didn't even hesitate. Sitting on a bench in the park, we each took the test. I was certain his would show he was softer than he liked to admit, and that it would get him to see the benefit of embracing his feminine side. I really wanted to say, "I told you so!"

When we both finished, I scored them. My score fell near the middle, but closer to the masculine side. His? I couldn't believe it. It was on the high end of ultra masculine. When he saw it, he shot up from the bench, flexed his muscles, and grunted, "Huh!" I laughed so hard I fell off the bench and onto the grass. We held each other and laughed until our stomachs hurt.

# 15
## JUDGMENT DAY

Religions are different roads converging to the same point. What does it matter that we take a different road, so long as we reach the same goal. Wherein is the cause for quarreling?

— MAHATMA GANDHI, *HIND SWARAJ*

I graduated from ORU in May 2011 and soon after joined Papa on a trip to visit an old acquaintance in Chicago. The man had been a protégé of Oral Roberts himself, and like Papa, he'd made quite a name for himself in the conservative Christian world. Like Papa, our pastor friend founded his own ministry that drew thousands of followers to his church in Tulsa on Sundays, and thousands more to the annual conference of music and ministry he held at the university every year. He was at the pinnacle of the evangelical hierarchy. Then, one night, as he watched a documentary on the genocide in Rwanda, he had an epiphany. Hell wasn't some biblical place of eternal torment. It was created right here on earth by depraved human behavior. He began to reject his strict fundamentalist beliefs in favor of more Universalist views. He sermonized about inclusion. Jesus, he said, was everyone's savior, not just the savior of Christians who claimed they were saved. In the end, all sins would be forgiven and all people would be reconciled with God. Because of his new beliefs, the evangelical order turned their backs on him. Some called him a heretic. His parishioners left his church in droves. But I adored him.

The visit with our friend went really well. I was surprised that Papa seemed to be developing a stronger relationship with the man. It was the only friendship I'd ever seen him develop with a person who, in his eyes, wasn't a true Christian, not anymore. "I really like that you're becoming good friends with him," I told Papa when we left the man. Papa nodded affirmatively and smiled.

Our conversation started again when we boarded the plane for home. I was going on and on about how much I liked our friend, how inspiring, how brilliant he was, and those kinds of things. I supposed Papa had been holding his tongue all along, and just couldn't do it any longer, because he made a remark about the man's not being saved. I was enraged.

"It's always like that with you, isn't it?" I said through clenched teeth. "Is there any point at which you will just judge people based on the fact that they're good human beings? It seems as though you can't be friends with anyone who isn't a Christian, and when you are nice to anyone who isn't a Christian you always have an end game."

I couldn't stop. The words spilled out as if I was puking them up. It was as if I was regurgitating every hurt, every fear, everything I had been holding back my entire life. The truth was that my faith, what was left of it, much more resembled our pastor friend's faith than my father's. If Papa couldn't accept our friend, how could he accept me? The answer was, he couldn't, which was precisely why I had been living a lie for most of my life. Why I had never let on about my crisis of faith. Why I had split into two people, the real Hannah and the Hannah my parents insisted I be. It didn't matter that they were true to their faith. That they believed in the literal word of the Bible. That they believed that only a relatively chosen few would be allowed into Heaven and everyone else would be ban-

164

ished to Hell. I didn't believe what they believed. I didn't know what I believed anymore, or even *if* I believed.

"You're always playing the game, Papa," I said, choking back tears. Mine were tears of rage. "This game of trying to save souls so they won't burn, and that's all you can experience of people, and that's all they can experience of you."

My father had been quiet to that point. But I had struck a nerve.

"You're exactly right!" he shot back. "That is my goal! With him! With everyone! Would you want *your* friends to burn in Hell?"

"Who do you think you are?" I cried. "Are you God?"

"If they're not saved they're not going to Heaven," Papa said.

There it was again. What I'd been hearing my whole life. It was always us against them. Those of us who have been saved and everyone else. I had never thought of my father as a "turn or burn" guy before, and I didn't like thinking it now.

"There's us then there's the rest of the world, isn't there, Papa?" I said. "Can't you accept that just because people don't believe in God in the way you do, that God still loves them? Can't you accept that it's possible that God loves everyone? Not just us?

That maybe all sin is forgivable and, in the end, we will all be saved?"

"That's not what the Bible says," Papa said.

I felt sick. "While we're at it, are gay people and Muslims on the 'they' side?" I asked. It was a rhetorical question, of course. I knew what Papa's answer would be. "You can't see the beauty in people, can you, Papa?" I cried. "You can't even see the beauty of God that is within your wonderful friend. He has been so good to you. He has been such a kind and loyal friend. Why can't you just see that?"

Papa wouldn't budge. "Yes, he is," he said. "But he isn't saved."

Fed up, I took a leap of faith and confessed my struggle. "Papa," I said. "I have felt my entire life that I have been bouncing back and forth from us to them, us to them, because I've never been accepted in the 'us' category. I tried my hardest to be accepted into your Christianity, and it just hasn't worked. Now I've studied theology, and I see these things on a broader perspective. Can't you see that you've built a wall between people who are like you and people who are not like you? That it doesn't have to be them and us?"

I don't know what I was expecting. Did I

think Papa would suddenly see things differently? Did I think he would question his core beliefs, to which he had devoted his entire adult life, because of one conversation with me? If I had been expecting to hear some kind of compromise, some acknowledgment that even though his friend didn't believe exactly as he did, he was still a good man and God could still love him, I would have been sorely disappointed. If I had such expectations. But I didn't. I knew exactly how Papa would respond.

"It *is* us and them," he said, "If you're not for us, you're against us!" He sounded like George W. Bush talking about the war on terrorists, and I guess in his good and evil way of thinking, it was the same thing.

I pushed back harder. "If it's a them-versus-us culture, I'd prefer to be one of them, thank you very much," I said bitterly.

Papa opened his book and pretended to read.

I turned to the window and pretended to doze off.

We were at an impasse. We were never going to agree. I thought he probably didn't even like me very much anymore. I was sure he was praying for my lost soul.

That's why I was so shocked when, the

following month, he asked me to join his staff.

# 16
## BACK TO THE FUTURE

A week is more than enough time for us to decide whether or not to accept our destiny.

— PAULO COELHO,
*THE DEVIL AND MISS PRYM*

I was working in Designer Women's Apparel at Saks Fifth Avenue in Tulsa that summer when Papa called to say he had something important to discuss with me. "I'll call you on my break," I promised. I couldn't imagine what couldn't wait until I clocked out of work at six, but Papa had insisted time was of the essence.

An hour later, during my break, I dialed Papa on my cell phone. "What's going on?" I asked. "Is everything okay?" Papa sounded excited, but he often sounded like that. Sometimes I thought he was an enthusiasm addict. "Remember when you told me there was nothing you wouldn't do to get to your goals?" he asked, a little bit mysteriously, for effect.

I thought that's what I had been doing. The job at Saks was one of three part-time jobs I was working since graduating from ORU that spring. I was also waitressing nights at two different Italian restaurants downtown to be able to support myself and pay for my first semester of graduate school at Oklahoma State for psychology. On Sundays, I worked as a sort of youth counselor at a local church (where yet another pastor was under fire for having an affair, this one with his nanny). That put a few extra dollars in my pocket each week, too, but I still was barely getting by. What was Papa getting at? Did I remember saying that about getting to my goals? "Yeee-aaah, I remember," I answered, tentatively.

A few months earlier, before our clash on the plane, which, by the way, was never spoken of again (evangelicals are often passive-aggressive and come at you through a side door, and that's what Papa was doing now), I had expressed my frustration to Papa over the phone that I was working my tail off but was barely able to buy groceries after bills. The job at Saks paid a small base salary, plus commission, which was where you made the real money, but it took time to build up a clientele, and I had only been on the job for five months. Papa taught us that money didn't bring happiness (yes, only God could do that), but I wanted at least to be able to support myself and not depend on a man to take care of me — the way everyone was telling me I should. I didn't just want to make a difference. I wanted to be able to make enough money to do the things I loved to do while I was changing the world. So Papa sent me a book about the psychology of selling. After I read it I immediately noticed a spike in my sales, but it wasn't enough to carry me through grad school for another semester.

I breathed into the phone, waiting for Papa's next move. "Well," he said, drawing his sentence out for suspense. "I have a proposal for you." *Oh, boy,* I said to myself, not to Papa.

Papa always had trouble keeping his assistants. Most of them were from Teen Mania, and although their intentions were good, they weren't equipped to do the complicated work it took to run his life. We were always hearing that this one wasn't smart enough, and that one was overqualified and left for a better-paying job, and someone else screwed up and was fired. It was always something. Papa is a kind man, but I knew he was a perfectionist and a tough taskmaster. It takes a lot of grit and dedication to push a ministry of that size forward. His schedule was rigorous, and sometimes even I couldn't keep up with him. Not only that, but Teen Mania's business office was operating in a time warp. The database was so outdated that the mission recruiting staff was calling people who had died years earlier, and they were still using file cabinets instead of computers to keep records. "I'd like to offer you a job as my executive assistant," Papa said.

Papa had the best of intentions, and he was a loving parent to me growing up. But he had a hard time letting go, and I knew that, after the conversation on the plane coming back from visiting his friend in Chicago, he feared not just that he and mom were losing me, but that I had lost my belief in their God. Offering me the job back in Texas was a smart move on his part, because I was competent and hard-working, and I certainly knew my scriptures. But I suspected that part of his motive (that passive-aggressive thing) was getting me back home so he could try to influence me back to his version of faith.

As I held the phone to my ear, a million thoughts swirled around in my head. I was in trouble financially. I wanted to finish grad school. I wanted to stay in Tulsa. As much as I loved my family, the last thing I wanted was to go back home to Garden Valley. "Well, Papa," I said. "Thank you for offering me the job. I will consider it."

Papa wasn't going to let me off the hook that easily. He said he needed an answer soon. His calendar was jam-packed with tours and missions and speaking gigs, and he needed someone now. He needed *me* now. "Okay," I said. "I promise I'll let you know soon."

I hung up and scolded myself. *Hannah, are you crazy? Have you lost your mind? Why didn't you just say no?* I did what I always did when I was in a panic. I called Austin and Garrett. What am I going to do? I cried. "C'mon over," Garrett said.

After work that night, we all met at Garrett's house, and over beers at his kitchen table, my friends laid out the pros and cons of my moving back to Texas. They, better than anyone who knew me, understood my struggles with Papa and my bewilderment over religion. I had gotten to the point that I didn't know where, or even if, it had a place in my life. I was sure Austin and Garrett would confirm what my instincts were screaming at me and give me all kinds of reasons to stay in Tulsa, then help me find a way to turn down the job gracefully. But they didn't do that.

Austin and Garrett avoided the cons and ticked off the pros. It didn't have to be a forever job, they said. I could go for six months, help Papa get things organized, learn a lot from him, save up some money, and move on. I would be able to travel with Papa, and who wouldn't want to do that? And I'd be living at home with no bills to pay. Make a list of demands, they said. First and foremost, insist on adequate pay, followed by a commitment that I'd get to travel with him, and I'd have weekends off to come back to Tulsa for classes and to spend time with my friends. I thought it over for five minutes, took a last sip of my beer, and headed for the door.

When I got home, I called Papa with my list of demands. He shot down my asking price. I accepted anyway.

# 17
## BACK TO TEEN MANIA

Extending from Biblical analogies and characters used as role models, the campaign has used narratives, metaphor and scripted staged presentations including images of weapons, pervasive use of a red pennant, and terms from a war lexicon such as "God's Army," "enemy" and "battle." It has used current and former members of the U.S. armed forces prominently in the Battle Cry stadium events, encouraging young people to become "the warriors in this battle." In "Battle Cry for a Generation," a book released at the start of the campaign, Ron Luce wrote, "This is war. And Jesus invites us to get into the action, telling us that the violent — the 'forceful' ones — will lay hold of the kingdom."

— CHRIS HEDGES,
*AMERICAN FASCISTS: THE CHRISTIAN RIGHT AND THE WAR ON AMERICA*

I had nine tan metal file cabinets in my office at Teen Mania. The kind people used in the eighties, before computers ran businesses. They'd been there as long as Papa, and so had some of the contents. Drawers were packed with random sheets of paper and manila folders that had obviously been recycled as many times as they had subjects crossed off them. Nothing was in order. I quickly learned what it would have been like to run a nonprofit as a young executive in the early '80s.

It wasn't anyone's fault. Papa had some great people on his staff, but the focus wasn't and had never been business, it was saving souls. In fact, the qualifications he looked for in job applicants didn't necessarily include college or even any business experience. Even on the ministry's website, it says employees are chosen first and foremost for their strong character and leadership. "They are individuals who have a passion for teenagers and missions and are committed to investing their lives into moving forward the Great Commission through ministering to this young generation," it says. Those traits didn't always translate into good business practices, and Teen Mania was proof of it.

Papa had ministered to millions of teens

and their families during his twenty-five years in the business, and I swear he had at least some information on every one of them that was all stuffed into those metal file drawers. And that was just the file cabinets in my office. Every office looked the same way. The database was in worse shape than the files. A lot of our program enrollments depended on phone solicitations by staffers using call lists that weren't updated regularly. The lists were supposed to be separated by category, but oftentimes the same person would get four or five calls from us, each pushing a different program. There were lots of times when someone would call a name on the list, only to be told that the person they were trying to reach had died years before. Phones were disconnected. People had moved away. But what could we do? People had to be called. Lives had to be changed.

Everywhere I looked I saw the effects of cutbacks and limited resources. Part of the problem was that the teenage interns did so much of the yeoman's work, and there were always turnovers and new people to train. Not just that, like most every major business, we were feeling the effects of a strained economy and had to make cuts in staffing, but at the same time the workload was increasing.

It was no secret that evangelical kids were abandoning their faith in droves (I was one of them) because they felt it was irrelevant to their lives. I had read the studies, and they all had similar results; something like three out of five felt disconnected from the church after they turned fifteen. Most of the kids who were surveyed said the faith they'd been raised with was suffocating and judgmental and out of step with their world. Many said they felt isolated in their struggles to live by outdated conservative Christian values when most of their peers were engaging in casual sex and enjoying forbidden music and videos and other "cultural garbage," as Papa called it. I knew Papa was worried about what he was seeing. He was even quoted in the *New York Times* about his fears, saying, "I'm looking at the data, and we've become post-Christian American, like post-Christian Europe. We've been working as hard as we know how to work — everyone in youth ministry is working hard — but we're losing."

I certainly understood why things were going the way they were. I was one of those young Christian casualties. But this was our audience, our bread and butter, and though I didn't agree with much of Papa's message anymore, I didn't want Teen Mania crippled or destroyed. I'd seen him commit his life to the ministry, and I knew his heart was right. And even if his methods hadn't worked for me, I saw him change lives for the better with his deep religious convictions and lively delivery. I'd witnessed kids toss away cigarettes and lighters and swear off alcohol, drugs, and sexual promiscuity after seeing him onstage. How could that be wrong?

I worked my puny rear end off. To say my job was challenging is almost funny, except that I usually fell into bed exhausted and crying after long twelve-hour days. I hated office work, but I saw some of Papa in me in that I expected a lot from the people who reported to me — most of them girls who were not much younger than me. I didn't accept mediocrity, and I was pretty demanding. The girls were expected to work hard, and their work had to be good. I gave some of them spelling and grammar tests I'd picked off the Internet before I'd allow them to start writing press releases for Papa's events, and I was a strict enforcer of time and tasks. I sure wouldn't have won any popularity contests. The girls who worked for me were always saying snarky things behind my back, which usually got back to me. In their eyes, I was a snob. I thought I was better and smarter than everyone else. I could boss them around just because I was Ron Luce's daughter. They got nothing but calloused hands for all of their hard work, and I had manicured nails and got everything I wanted.

I wished I could have told them what I was making, which, given the hours I was putting in on my own time, was less than minimum wage.

*Mom with me and baby Charity.*

*Papa driving me, Charity, and Cameron on the four-wheeler in our front yard.*

Mom and Papa with me as a baby.

Papa teaching me to play the guitar.

Me and Papa.

I was a flower girl in a Teen Mania alum's wedding. I was five.

The family outside the house in Tulsa, Oklahoma, where I was born. This was before we moved to Texas.

We love to
celebrate
birthdays, and
little Cammy loved
chocolate cake!

Summer always
meant fun in the
sun.

Here's me and
Charity holding dolls.
We liked to have tea
parties in the forest!
We were country
gals.

*Family
pyramid.*

*Jet skiing on our lake.*

An Acquire the Fire weekend. Thousands of young people attend every event. (Michael Mistretta, 2013)

People worshipping at Acquire the Fire. (Michael Mistretta, 2013)

*At my Oral Roberts University graduation.*

*Graduation 2011.*

In Paris with Papa in the summer of
2010. My father preached at a church in
Paris, and I came along for the ride!

The whole family.

Self portrait. These were the glasses I wore on the day of the accident.

Having fun in my office at Teen Mania Ministries.

This is how I decorated my office at Teen Mania Ministries.

This was taken an hour before we got to the plane, May 11, 2012.

I took this pic with Austin (left) and Garrett (on the right) before the plane took off.

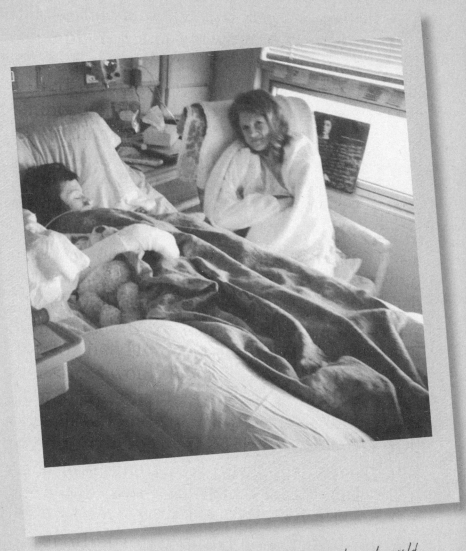

Mom stayed by my bedside at the hospital as much as she could.

Resting at the hospital. I had to have that bear every night before I went to sleep.

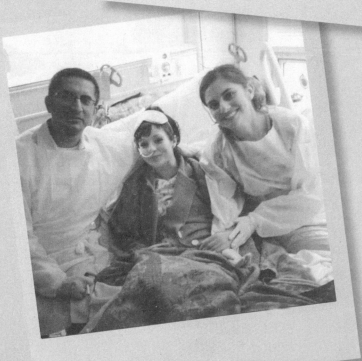

With the burn doctor in Kansas City who did my graft surgeries and my favorite nurse.

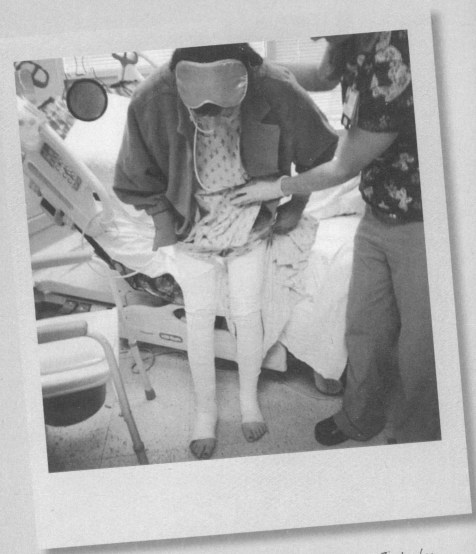

I had to get up and walk every day. This was the first time I stood up after my surgeries.

With fire chief
Duane Banzet
and Robin
Gaby Fisher.

Me and Mom.

# 18
## GARRETT'S ENGAGEMENT

Pierre, who had done more than any human being to draw her out of the caves of her secret, folded life, now threw her down into deeper recesses of fear and doubt. The fall was greater than she had ever known, because she had ventured so far into emotion and had abandoned herself to it.
— ANAÏS NIN, *DELTA OF VENUS*

I had been back in Texas for three months when Austin told me that Garrett was engaged. I was stunned and angry. "Engaged?" I cried. "When did that happen? Why didn't he tell me?" I'd been back to Tulsa five or six times since I left, and I usually saw both Garrett and Austin during those weekends. Garrett never said anything to me about getting engaged.

I knew he was dating, and there wasn't anything I could say about that. We were in different places in our lives. He was twenty-nine, and he'd been saying for some time that he felt like he needed to get married. Austin called it an early midlife crisis. He said Garrett was worried that the life he'd been raised to see for himself, a life that included a wife and kids and a house with a yard, was slipping away. I was twenty-two, and that was the last thing I wanted at that point in my life. I had made it really clear to Garrett that I was unwilling to make a lifetime commitment to him or anyone else. The thought of marriage terrified me. I wasn't ready, and I didn't expect him to wait around forever while I was out catching my dreams. But we were so connected, and he had intentionally kept his big news from me. "He said not to tell you!" Austin said. "But you're my friend, too, and I thought you should know." I felt so betrayed.

Austin said he was worried about Garrett. He thought he was acting impulsively and that he would have married whoever came up to bat. He wondered if we should do an intervention, to try to get him to see the error of his ways, but we both agreed that was risky. We didn't want Garrett to get angry and cut us out of his life.

My bimonthly Tulsa weekend was coming

up, and I called Garrett, as usual, to tell him I'd be there. We made arrangements to meet that Saturday night near Oklahoma State University, in Stillwater, a two-hour drive west of Tulsa, where he'd been teaching business classes. It would be just the two of us. I didn't say anything about Austin's telling me about the engagement, and he didn't mention it. He said he couldn't wait to see me.

My stomach hurt the whole way from Texas to Oklahoma. I arrived in Tulsa late Friday afternoon and settled in with my girlfriend Pam, whom I was staying with. I couldn't get to sleep that night. "What am I going to say when I see him?" I asked myself as I pulled up the covers and threw them off again. Did I have the right to say anything? Did he have the right not to? Garrett and I had jumped from friendship to romance and back again more times than I could count over the two years we'd known each other. We dated, but it never really felt like a traditional relationship. We enjoyed each other's company so much and we loved spending time together, but there hadn't been guidelines or boundaries. If I took a stand now, would it look as if I wanted more? Did I want more? All I knew was I didn't want to lose him. I knew

Garrett and I knew he went into hiding when he was cornered or challenged. What if I confronted him and he walked out of my life? I couldn't imagine my life without him.

But he'd lied to me. He'd say he didn't lie because he hadn't said anything. But it was a lie by omission. Sooner or later, something had to be said. But when, and what? I didn't know what to do. All the next afternoon I tried to prepare myself for what might happen. The best-case scenario would be if he said something to me before I had to bring it up. "Hey, Hannah! I have good news!" Knowing Garrett the way I did, I couldn't imagine he'd do that. He hated hurting people, and he knew I'd be hurt that he hadn't let on how serious his dating relationship had become in a few short months.

It took longer than it should have to get to Stillwater; I dawdled, stopping every fifteen minutes for gas or for water or to use a public restroom. As I was stalling, Garrett was texting me, asking where I was. He was excited to see me. When did I think I'd be there? What was taking so long? The tone of his messages made me angry. What was a man who was engaged doing talking to another girl that way? I put myself in the other girl's place. It felt bad.

My hair was brushed in long curls, and my makeup was perfect. We met at our favorite place near the college. He hugged me really tight, and we lingered in each other's arms for a moment. I thought maybe he was holding on because he knew it would be our last time together this way. "How *are* you?" I said, pulling back and looking up at him. He looked so handsome in his Oxford button-down shirt and khakis, very professorial. I liked that. "You look great!" I said. "And," he said, "you look beautiful." What I didn't say was that I had never seen him looking so dead tired.

Garrett was always telling me how pretty I was and how brilliant I was. I loved that about him. He seemed so proud of me. I wasn't used to that. "I've missed you," I said. "Me, too," he said. We talked about many things over the next hour or so. Movies and books. His doctoral dissertation, his teaching job and how much he loved it. My Teen Mania experiences. We were having such a wonderful time together that I didn't want anything to change. I wanted to pretend it was last week, before Austin broke the news to me, but I knew I couldn't do that. "So what's new with you?" I asked gently, hoping that would open the door for him to tell me he was engaged and, the next minute, hoping he wouldn't and I could just forget for the night.

Garrett's dad had been hospitalized a couple of weeks earlier, and he was in bad shape. He'd been working in an oil field when a piece of the machinery toppled, cracking him in the head and causing his brain to swell, and his prognosis wasn't good. Garrett told me that, during the week, Papa had come to the hospital to pray over his dad. I knew Papa was going to be in town, and had asked him to visit the hospital, but I didn't know he had. Garrett said he'd sat at his dad's bedside for hours before Papa got there, and his father had been completely unresponsive, as he had since the accident. That same day, the doctors told the family he might never speak or think again. It was a terrible time for them.

The doctors had barely left the room, Garrett said, when Papa swept in with his powerful presence, laid his hands over his father, and prayed for his full recovery. Garrett, of course, loved Papa. He idolized him, I should say. The man crush, remember? He said the energy in the room was charged. He was watching the scene play out, and he'd been shocked to see his father's eyes flutter open and widen, as he looked straight at Papa. His father closed

186

his eyes again, but that had been the first and only time he'd reacted to anything since he was injured. I got chills when he told me the story.

When he finished talking, he leaned in to kiss me, but I pulled back. "What's wrong?" he asked. I didn't respond, and he seemed puzzled. He pulled me closer, and I turned my face away, wondering whether it was time to say something. I know what he was thinking. He thought I was toying with him again. He'd accused me of doing that in the past. *I know you want me, but you can never have me.* I saw that he was getting impatient with me. His face was flushed red, and he pursed his lips. "Hannah," he said. "You know what I'm going through with my dad. Why are you . . ."

I touched his arm and looked him in the eyes. "Garrett," I said, interrupting him. "I'm really sorry about what you're going through. I'm not playing a game here. There's nothing I would rather do than kiss you. You know how much I care about you. But you haven't been honest with me."

He looked sincerely taken aback. "What do you mean?" he asked.

"I mean your engagement," I said plaintively.

He leaned back. I knew his instinct was to

run away. I desperately wanted to talk it through before he shut down, shut me out, but it was already too late. I could see it in his eyes. He turned away from me, dismissing me. I tried to engage him. "Garrett," I said, pleading. "If this is the person for you, I support it. I want you to be happy. But why wouldn't you have given me the respect of telling me? I had to find out from Austin. Do you understand how much that hurt me?"

I felt such a mix of emotions. I wanted to tell him to forget what had just happened. I wished I could have said we could go on being the way we were no matter what else happened. But I also wanted him to honor the commitment he made to someone else, and I wanted to respect his decision enough to hold him to that commitment, as least as it concerned me. I told him I refused to be that second girl people talked about. That girl who had to hide under the bed. I had too much integrity and self-respect to play that role in anyone's life.

What I didn't say was that I knew he couldn't be my friend anymore. His wish had always been that some day I would be ready to share my life with him. He had been biding his time, being my friend, doing things my way, but now his dream of being with me was being replaced with someone else, and I had found out. I wasn't about to feel responsible for his guilt, and I wasn't going to play second to anyone. "I'm sorry, Garrett," I said sadly.

He was hurt and wouldn't speak. The silence was uncomfortable and then unbearable. I grabbed my bag and said I was leaving and driving back to Tulsa. He didn't try to stop me. "I'm going to go now, and I'd like to continue this conversation when it's not the middle of the night and we can be clear-headed," I said. I searched his face for some sign that he was on the same page as me, that he was willing to talk it out, too. All I saw was sadness. "We'll talk about this in the morning?" I asked. He shook his head yes, but I wasn't at all sure he'd call.

While I was still in my car, he texted me. He said he really believed in me and he would be hoping for my dreams to come true and cheering my future from afar. It was a sweet and somber message. I feared it was good-bye and that he was cutting me out of his life. I read it again, and my heart sank. I questioned with regret our conversation but, at the same time, I was glad I had taken a stand. He had to make a choice. But what if he didn't choose me? We would never have our late-night movies together, or our walks by the river, or our talks in the park. It would really be over. I began to realize just how much I valued him, how much he meant to me.

But I was afraid it was too late.

# 19
# BACK IN TEXAS

Life calls the tune, we dance.
— JOHN GALSWORTHY, *FIVE TALES*

I was so lonely in Texas. Even when I did have free time, my friends were all four hours away in Tulsa. I hadn't been back since my confrontation with Garrett two months earlier and, just as I'd feared, he hadn't contacted me. When I needed a good pep talk, I'd call or Skype Austin. He'd update me on Garrett's engagement (the wedding was planned for that December) and he'd pick me up by telling me funny stories about ORU.

By then, Austin was talking marriage with Elizabeth (he assured me that she didn't care about designer handbags or drive a yellow Mustang). I liked her the first time I met her. She told me a funny story about how their romance began: "He told me I was going to give him his number when we met. I said, 'Why would I do that?' He said, 'So we can communicate.' " I had to laugh. That was Austin.

Elizabeth was smart and down to earth and beautiful, of course, maybe even more so inside than outside. She had a strong Christian faith, as Austin did, but not that in-your-face kind of faith that I had learned to dislike. He was so in love with her. I'd never seen him so happy. His edge was gone. Being with Elizabeth had softened him. I noticed the residual anger he felt from his childhood and the war seemed to have melted away. She was no pushover, that's for sure. She'd laid down the law right from the start. "If you're ever unfaithful, I'm gone. No questions asked. No second chances." She was independent and free-spirited, but she worshipped him, and even more important in my eyes, she endorsed our friendship. I wasn't surprised when he told me he'd bought her a ring.

One day that spring, after a particularly challenging time at the ministry, I called Austin looking for moral support. He and Garrett and I had often talked together about our futures, and they always made everything sound exciting and not stressful. I had driven to one of my favorite spots in the countryside and rolled out a blanket in the middle of the field and pretended Austin was sitting next to me. "I made a mistake, coming back to Texas," I said. I told Austin that the job wasn't what I thought it would be. I wasn't traveling, and I was stuck in an office all day. The place was a mess and the Internet was forever crashing and no one knew anything about computer maintenance. I missed my friends, and I was going out of my mind. If I never saw another Christian teenager in my life it would be fine by me.

Austin chuckled. "You knew what you were getting yourself into," he said. "We talked about all of this before you left. This is a chance for you to get close to your family again and to save up some money so you can go to Europe like you want to. C'mon. It's not forever. Buck up, Luce!"

The sun warmed my face, and hearing his happy voice seemed to diminish the troubles of the workday, and my complaints about gossipy teenagers and dusty files seemed suddenly small. "So what about you?" I asked.

Austin said he and Elizabeth had set a wedding date for the summer of the following year, in August. He was graduating in a month with a business degree and, even though he had been a stellar student, and he would have been a catch for any business, he was worried about getting a job. The job market was discouraging. He and Garrett had been tossing around ideas for their own business, and some of their prospects looked pretty promising, but nothing was concrete. He needed a steady income, especially now that he had found his future wife.

I was telling Austin about how I was worried for Papa's ministry because of what all the studies about young evangelicals were showing. There were other problems, too. Two of his directors had recently resigned, and quality candidates weren't exactly knocking down the door to apply for average-paying jobs in a rural fundamentalist Christian community. My long-term plan didn't have Teen Mania in it, despite the fact that he and Austin always said I'd be a natural replacement for Papa when and if he ever decided to retire. I never understood why they thought that I could or would want to fill that role.

I'm not sure how the subject came up, but I told Austin that if he got really desperate and couldn't find a job, I could always get him one with me at Teen Mania. I was half joking. I never thought he'd consider something like that, after hearing about my experience there, but he jumped at it. "You'd do that, Hannah?" he bellowed. "Really?" He sounded so excited. I wondered if he was being sarcastic. But he began ticking off all of the things he could do to help make sure Teen Mania stayed afloat. "You don't know what you're saying," I said. "I'm his daughter, and I'm working sixty hours a week." Austin was unfazed. He had studied business and had an entrepreneur's mind, he said. He could bring fresh ideas to it, and he wasn't afraid of hard work.

I found myself wanting to jump up and down. I didn't want to get my hopes up, but the idea of working with Austin for the remainder of my time at Teen Mania, even if it was only for a few months, was thrilling. I truly believed he had a lot to offer Papa, and he'd grown up in rural Oklahoma, so he wouldn't be in culture shock moving to the country. "If you send me your resume, I'll talk to my dad," I said.

He emailed me his resume that same day, and I passed it along to Papa, who happened to be in town. Papa knew something about Austin. I'd been talking him up for a long time, and he was excited about the possibility of bringing him on board. He was impressed with Austin's patriotism and military credentials and his commitment to his schooling and, most of all, his faith. It didn't hurt that I told him I thought Austin was like him in that both of them were idealists and visionaries. Papa liked that.

Austin didn't know that Papa was pretty much already sold on him when he called to ask him to come to Texas for an interview. Since two of Papa's top people had recently stepped down, he wanted to meet Austin in person to get a feel for which job would be best for him. I told him that Austin would be a great asset, no matter which position he took.

Papa and Austin only spoke for a few minutes on the phone, but the conversation was easy between them. Both of them were personable and straightforward and, even though Austin respected Papa's place in the evangelical world, he wasn't intimidated by his position or his power, the way Garrett and others were.

They had only spoken for a few minutes on the phone when Papa asked Austin, "So when can you come for a talk and tour?"

Austin didn't hesitate. "I can be there this week if you want, sir," he said.

"Great," Papa said. "I'm looking forward to meeting you."

"Me, too, sir," Austin said.

I was beside myself with excitement when I heard Austin was really coming. I missed him terribly, and I couldn't wait to see him again. He said he'd be there on Friday. "This is a dream come true!" I said when he told me.

And that's how the nightmare started.

# 20
## DESTINY

Surely if we knew what bitterness fate held in store, we would shrink back in fear and let the cup of life pass us by untasted.

— JACQUELINE CAREY,
*KUSHIEL'S DART*

Austin was nervous about meeting Papa. He'd seen him onstage at an Acquire the Fire event back when he was a kid, but they'd never officially met. He must have called me five times a day asking for tips. What should he say? What not to say? "First and foremost, no cussing," I said. "And get it across that you have a strong relationship with God."

"I think I can handle that," he said in his Oklahoma country boy twang. I could hear the smile on his face. Even though I knew Papa would fall in love with Austin, I was nervous for him. Papa wasn't just some guy he needed to impress. He was a serious

198

man of God.

Austin was scheduled to come to Texas for his in-person meeting on that following Friday. I knew it was a hectic time for Austin. He was graduating that weekend, and he'd told me he was struggling with his senior business presentation, which had to be finished before he walked. Nothing could stop Austin from getting what he wanted, though, and he wanted the job with Papa at Teen Mania.

He planned to drive from Tulsa that Friday morning, spend the day with Papa at Teen Mania, and return home that same night in time to wrap up his business final. I was excited for his visit and over the moon about the prospect of his coming to Texas to work with us. I was screeching into the phone the night before. "You're coming! I can't believe you're coming!" He had so much to offer Papa and Teen Mania, and I was dying to have my wonderful friend nearby. It would be just like the old days.

Austin called late on Thursday night to let me know he was packed up and ready to roll at sunup. I reiterated the rules. No swearing. No God jokes. Be careful what you say and, even more important, be mindful of how you say it. You've got to sound humble, I said. God frowned upon people who bragged. In the Bible, the boasters are listed among the wicked of men. "And the people at Teen Mania will hold it against you," I said. "You're not making this any easier," he said. We both laughed. "I know, Hannah. I know," he said. "Oh, by the way, Garrett is coming with me."

He could have been saying, "By the way, I just got my car washed," or, "By the way, the weather's supposed to be nice." But, Garrett is coming? The butterflies I had felt in my stomach over Austin's visit suddenly felt like birds flapping around my insides. "What?" I cried. "What do you mean Garrett's coming? Why is Garrett coming?" Austin knew all about what had happened between Garrett and me. He knew I hadn't heard from Garrett for two months, not a word since our confrontation, and he knew how I felt about the whole engagement thing. Yet he'd invited Garrett without even telling (or asking) me first. I was beside myself. This was something my dad would do.

I always said that in some ways Austin reminded me of Papa, except that he was more fun. He knew social etiquette, but he overstepped it whenever he felt like it, and he was so charming he could get away with it. Darn him! "Austin!" I cried. "Why is he coming? There's no reason you need a chaperon for your job interview." I know Austin thought I was overreacting. "I don't know!" he said. "I don't know, but he won't stop talking about you. He won't shut up! He even offered to pay for the gas for the trip. He's crazy about you, Hannah. You know he is." Then why was he marrying someone else? I hadn't heard any news about a broken engagement or a change of wedding plans. The last thing I'd heard was that Garrett and his fiancée had just bought a house together, and the wedding plans were chugging right along. Under the circumstances, it was easier not seeing him. What was the point? It could only complicate things for us both.

Needless to say, I didn't get any sleep that night.

They arrived earlier than scheduled on Friday morning. I had gone to get my passport renewed in Tyler because I was scheduled to travel with Papa to Mexico, and I wasn't around when they got there. I'd tried calling Austin on my way back from Tyler to see what their estimated time of arrival was, but there wasn't any cell service between Tyler and Garden Valley, so I drove straight to Teen Mania.

When I heard they were already there, I

201

went to find them. Austin was already interviewing with Papa, so I went looking for Garrett and found him hanging out with some of his buddies from the ministry. Garrett was a bit of a legend at Teen Mania. He'd gotten to know a lot of the kids when he'd joined them on mission trips in the past, and many of them worshipped him. He was reveling in the attention of his fans when he first saw me. It was an awkward moment, and he was sheepish at first. I wasn't sure what to say, but I knew I couldn't say too much in front of everyone who was there. "Let's go back to my parents' house so we can make some coffee," I said.

Garrett had never been to my house before. It's very peaceful there. The house sits on a lake at the end of a private lane with lots of trees. He loved the setting. We brewed a pot of coffee and took the steaming mugs down to the dock by the lake. Garrett still wasn't saying much, and my words seemed stuck in my throat. I tried to think of something to make things less awkward. I stifled the urge to ask him about his wedding plans. "Let's go fishing," I said instead.

Garrett said he was game. I'm sure he was as relieved as I was for the distraction. I ran up to the house and pulled a couple of poles out of the garage, and we dug in the soil by the lake for worms. I made him put the worms on our hooks, and we cast our lines into the lake. "It's beautiful here," he said. He sounded melancholy.

I guess it was me who brought up Austin. I was telling Garrett that I worried if Austin took the job he'd be overwhelmed, as I was, because there was so much work to do to make the ministry current. He said he was worried, too, and thought Austin was getting in over his head and couldn't handle the executive position he wanted because he'd never run anything before. I think Garrett was feeling left out and probably jealous that Austin had the flexibility to be able to come to Texas and join the ministry, *Garrett's* ministry, the one that had changed his life. "He'll be overwhelmed, and I'll have to help him," Garrett said.

I'm not sure at what point in the conversation it happened, but I noticed that the tension that had been separating us had eased. Garrett had inched closer to me on the dock, and we weren't watching for fish to tug on our lines to avoid looking at each other anymore.

Garrett's voice turned quiet. He dropped his head and said his engagement wasn't going well, and he was sad about that. He wasn't happy in the relationship, and he was pretty sure she wasn't either. In fact, he said, he'd found a "Dear Garrett" letter she'd been composing on her computer that said as much. They'd been trying to work through their differences, he said, but he was feeling torn about what he wanted. "I really don't know what I want to do or where I want to be," he said.

Garrett could be a bit of a drama queen, especially when it came to love and relationships, but I could tell this was weighing heavily on him. "What are you going to do?" I asked gently. "Will you go through with the wedding anyway?" Garrett hesitated for a moment, then turned to look at me. "Do you think it would be good for me to come to Teen Mania?" he asked.

He caught me completely off guard with his question. I didn't know what to say. I never expected that from Garrett. He was already hugely successful in his career, and had recently taken a full-time job as an assistant professor at Northeastern State University, about twenty minutes outside of Tulsa. He was earning more than one hundred thousand dollars a year with a bright future in academia. Teen Mania paid a fraction of that, and he'd be giving up his university career. I was afraid he was thinking about coming to Texas to escape from his wedding plans and because Austin and I would be right there to help him pick up the pieces. Yet I knew that neither Austin nor I would be long-termers at Teen Mania. The last thing I wanted was for Garrett to one day look back on his decision and blame me for letting him make a huge mistake at such a vulnerable point in his life. As much as I may have selfishly wanted to shout out, "Yes! Come! We'll all be together again!" I couldn't.

I said, "You know my experiences here, Garrett. You know what it's been like for me. Of course, this is your decision to make. Only you know if this is something you really want to do. But Austin won't be here forever, and I won't be here much longer at all." I said that because I feared for myself, too. I was reassuring myself that I had made a commitment to Papa to stay a year and not a day longer, and I needed to keep that commitment. I had plans to finish graduate school, and I wanted to spend time in Europe. I didn't want to paint myself into a corner and not be able to get out of Garden Valley.

As I was talking, I realized this was the first time I had felt nervous around Garrett, that kind of jittery, insecure nervousness you feel when you realize you like a boy and care what he's thinking about you. I was hoping Garrett would figure out what it was he was feeling as we hashed things out. I sensed there was something he was holding back, something he wanted to say but couldn't, and part of me wanted to hear what I suspected it was. But I waited for words that didn't come.

Papa hired Austin on the spot. It was a no-brainer, he said. Papa was taken with Austin's confidence, as well as his leadership style. Austin told him how he'd motivated young Marine recruits, and that he could do the same for Teen Mania. He was a team builder and pulled people in. He was gregarious, his handshake was strong, and he looked you in the eye when he talked to you. "A man's man," Papa had called him. Austin was going to become his new director of marketing operations. I squealed with excitement.

After the interview, Papa brought Austin back to the house, and he and Garrett got a tour of what I call the Hall of Shame, the hallway in our house with pictures of me at every awkward stage of my adolescence. I saw the handwriting on the wall. I would be odd man out. The men seemed to be bonding at my expense, but I understood. It was a man thing. I was just happy they all got along so well. (I wasn't so happy when I found out that Austin was going to make significantly more than what I made.) Papa told Austin he wanted him to start work the following Thursday, right after his graduation from ORU. His start date was May 10, 2012. His first official role as marketing director would be to attend Papa's Acquire the Fire season finale, which was being held in Council Bluffs, Iowa, that next weekend.

Austin and Garrett returned to Tulsa that night. A couple of days went by, and my cell phone rang at midnight one night. Garrett's number flashed on the screen. "Hi!" I said. "Why are you calling me so late?" He asked how I was and I told him that I'd been worried about my great-grandmother, whose health was failing. I had recently spoken to her on the phone, and she'd pleaded with me to visit in Colorado because she felt she didn't have long to live. I adored my great-grandmother. Garrett listened patiently the way he always did. But when he spoke he sounded anxious.

"I need to talk to you about a few things," he said. My heart skipped, the way it usually did when I was nervous. I was afraid (or did I hope?) that what he had to say was

207

about him and me.

"I need to know a few things," he said.

"Okay," I said, a little too quickly.

"I'm really considering going to work at Teen Mania," he said.

"Really?"

". . . But I have to make a certain amount of money. I could also work at a university nearby, and I've already looked into when they are going to be hiring a marketing professor."

He went on to say how important Teen Mania was to him and what a difference it had made to him growing up. He hadn't found a whole lot of things in life that really satisfied him, he said, but he knew that going to work for the ministry and helping to make it continue to be successful would be fulfilling. "I think this is something I really want to do, Hannah," he said.

"Wow," I said. "That's a big decision." I asked myself: *Is this his way of running away from his engagement? Is he looking for an excuse to get out of it, and this is his excuse?*

"Well," Garrett said, "I just don't know what I'm doing with my life. I just bought a house. I'm engaged for the fourth time. I can see my life. I'll get married. Have a couple of kids. Get tenure. What kind of life is that? Is that what my life is about? Getting tenure at a university?" He started choking up. "I want to do something that matters," he said, his voice shaking. "I want to make a difference!" I imagined his thoughts like a wad of paper. He was tossing them at me faster than I could catch what he was trying to say. "Garrett," I said, trying to calm him. "I have confidence that wherever you are, even if you are at a university, you will do whatever you want to do. Just because you have a house and these other things doesn't mean you can't make a difference. You can do that wherever you are."

I thought about something Austin had said. He told me that Garrett was really struggling. That he was trying to find a way to break off his engagement without having a breakdown himself. He said that Garrett wanted to be with me, but he wasn't sure about where he stood with me. I didn't know what to think about that. I still wasn't sure that I was open to the possibility of him and me, and unless and until he could tell me about how he was feeling about me, I probably wouldn't know. In the meantime, I had to be careful that I didn't get in the way of his decision about whether to go through with his wedding.

"Garrett," I said, trying to tread lightly.

"If it's really something else you're talking about here, we can talk about that, too."

Garrett was quiet. I could hear the struggle in his silence.

I said, "I know you know how Teen Mania is. If you decide to come here, you'll be a very valuable asset, and there are a lot of good things you can do."

He was silent.

"Don't lie to yourself, Garrett," I said.

"I'm not, Hannah," he said. "I know what I want."

But if what he wanted was me, he didn't say.

NTSB Identification: CEN12FA290

14 CFR Part 91: General Aviation

Accident occurred Friday, May 11, 2012 in Chanute, KS

Aircraft: CESSNA 401, registration: N9DM.

The cross-country flight departed the Richard Lloyd Jones Jr. Airport (RVS), Tulsa, Oklahoma, approximately 1545, for the Council Bluffs Municipal Airport (CBF), Council Bluffs, Iowa.

Initial reports indicate that the pilot received air traffic control services and had requested to descend from 10,000 feet mean sea level (msl) to 8,000 feet msl.

There were no further radio communications between the pilot and air traffic control, nor were there any distress calls by the pilot. — National Transportation Safety Board preliminary report, May 18, 2012.

# 21
# THE CRASH

That was the day my whole world went black. Air looked black. Sun looked black. I laid up in bed and stared at the black walls of my house. . . . Took three months before I even looked out the window, see the world still there. I was surprised to see the world didn't stop.
— KATHRYN STOCKETT, *THE HELP*

Six of us were going to the youth rally in Council Bluffs. Austin and I were going for Teen Mania, and Garrett invited himself "just to hang out," he said, but Austin had told me it was so he could spend time with me. Besides the three of us, Austin invited his roommate from ORU, Stephen Luth, whom he had just recruited for Teen Mania's marketing team. He brought along another classmate, Stephen's housemate, Luke Sheets, who was our pilot. Austin's girlfriend, Elizabeth, was coming, too, and she was supposed to fly with us, but at the last minute her dad asked her to drive instead.

Before we decided to fly, we had all discussed driving to Iowa together, but when Stephen offered up the plane and Luke's services we accepted the offer figuring it would save time. On the drive from Texas to Tulsa to meet up with everyone, I felt anxious about the flight, but I told myself I was just being silly and pushed aside my fears.

We planned to take off from Jones Riverside Airport in Tulsa at one o'clock in the afternoon. I'd arrived in town late the previous evening. Early the next morning Austin and Stephen met me to help pack things still in storage from my college days that I would take back to Texas after the trip. When the U-Haul was loaded, the boys dropped me off at Stephen's apartment and then took the rented van and Austin's pickup truck to ORU to park for the weekend. Once back at the apartment, Austin realized he was missing his wallet. He didn't want to travel without it, which meant retracing all of his steps — the storage place, the campus lot, and McDonald's. I thought he'd be right back, but he was gone so long that I finished getting ready and was bored enough to take pictures of myself on my iPhone. Garrett called while I was waiting to ask if I needed anything from the store before we left. I giggled, excited about the idea of our trip, and told him to surprise me. Austin finally called and asked me to check his travel bag one more time and, sure enough, there was his wallet, tucked into a zip pocket. By then it was almost three o'clock in the afternoon.

Luke was waiting by the plane when Austin, Stephen, and I finally got to the airport. I watched from the tarmac as Luke did a preflight check on the airplane, a twin-engine Cessna 401. Luke was only twenty-four, but had already been flying for five years and had earned his commercial pilot's license two years earlier. Garrett was the last to arrive. I'd been texting him all morning with updates about our delayed departure. He pulled up in his shiny red Hummer just in time to board with us.

We were all dressed to impress. The boys wore button-down shirts and pressed trousers. I was in my mom's lacy burnt lavender blouse and chic red Lips sunglasses. "Ladies first," someone said. I climbed on board and headed to the back of the plane, to a seat facing forward. I'd flown in plenty of small planes during trips for Papa's ministry, and

I didn't like facing away from the cockpit and looking down as the plane rose into the sky. Garrett and Austin climbed in behind me and took seats facing me, with their backs to the cockpit. Stephen climbed in the front beside Luke. The engines rumbled to start, and Austin and I broke out the snacks we'd bought at the Whole Foods market on the way to the airport. We toasted with shots of "Dragon's Breath," an organic concoction of ginger root, lemon, and cayenne pepper. We had so much to celebrate. What better way than to spend a weekend with your best friends?

"Oh, my gosh!" I cried. "We're on vacation together! We're in the same hotel! We're going to have a *blast*!"

As excited as the rest of us were, Garrett was awkward and aloof, and I knew him well enough to sense that he was tied in knots about the idea of ending his relationship with his fiancée. I knew he felt bad for lying to me, too. He couldn't even look me in the eye. Austin had told me that Garrett only decided to join us when he heard I'd be on the plane. Perhaps he thought that being away together was a good opportunity to try to continue to mend our fractured friendship. I was hoping that once we were on our way, he would relax enough that we could talk about what was next for us, whatever that turned out to be.

As we waited to be cleared for takeoff, I tried lightening the mood. "I just realized we don't have any pictures together," I said, pulling my iPhone out of my purse. "We've got to have pictures." Austin and Garrett obliged, and we all leaned into each other and smiled. I snapped four shots. In each picture, we are all grinning from ear to ear.

It was three-forty-five when we finally took off, two hours and forty-five minutes later than our planned departure. The route would be a straight shot north, and around two hours long, so we would still make it to Council Bluffs in time for the Teen Mania youth rally at seven o'clock that evening. Austin and I could barely contain our excitement. We couldn't stop talking about our ideas for Papa's ministry and how much fun it would be working together.

About thirty minutes into the flight, just as I had hoped, Garrett began loosening up and looking at me when we were talking. When I pitched an idea for marketing the ministry, his eyes lit up, and he praised me, saying, "Hannah! That's brilliant!" The plane was chilly, and I was thinking about grabbing my jacket from behind me, when, just then, he switched seats to the one next to me. He said it was because the plane was loud and he wanted to be able to hear me better, but I knew he was trying to regain our normal closeness again, and I was happy about that.

Seeing Garrett that day made me realize how much I'd missed him and our long, intimate talks. I was so looking forward to our weekend together. I couldn't wait to land and get started. We were making good time to Council Bluffs. The weather was beautiful. The sky, blue and clear. As we flew over the patchwork quilt of Middle America, I leaned into Garrett and thought about how excited I was to be on this adventure with him. Everything felt so right.

Then something went terribly wrong.

Up front in the cockpit, I see Luke turn a knob on the control panel and I think it must be for the heater. At first, there is a terrible burning smell, and then a blast of scorching hot air shoots from the vents. I watch Luke fiddle with the knob again, but the heat still comes fiercely and relentlessly. The hot air blowing from the vents turns an ashy gray. The smelly swirls of smoke remind me of the Fiendfyre in Harry Potter. It's coming for us. I can see Luke at the controls, with his headphones on, talking to

Stephen, but I can't make out what they're saying. The smoke is blowing directly into Luke's face and I wonder how he can see anything. "What's going on?" I shout. I'm holding my blouse up to my mouth, trying in vain to stop myself from breathing in noxious fumes. No one answers.

The air in the plane is now stifling and grimy. My eyes burn and water and my cheeks are on fire. Garrett yells at me, "Get the water bottles!" There are eight bottles of water in a cooler behind me and I grab them, one by one, and toss them to Garrett and Austin. They fling the water from the open bottles at the heating vents, but smoke continues to pour into the cabin. Garrett runs to the back of the plane, grabs the fire extinguisher, and sprays it toward the cockpit. The scene is chaotic. Surreal. How can this be happening? The smoke is so dense in the cabin that I can barely make out Luke and Stephen up front anymore. Garrett and Austin are trying so hard to save us. And I have never felt so helpless.

Minutes feel like hours. There's a lot of shouting and screaming. Garrett pops open the door and tries to suck in some fresh air. For a moment, I think he's trying to jump out of the plane, and I consider following him out, but we're still really high in the air.

We are all getting tired. I can barely keep myself awake. My temples throb. Bile rises in my throat, and I fear I may throw up. Even with my foggy head I know we are being poisoned. So this is it? This is the end of our lives? We've hardly lived. I hear Luke shouting into the radio, asking for permission to descend. We're dropping fast. Stephen crawls back from the cockpit and sits on the floor facing me. "We're going to crash!" he cries. The plane banks right and then left. I look out the window, and my skin prickles with terror. We are headed straight down. The earth twirls below, a kaleidoscope of doom.

The strangest things pop into your mind when death intrudes on your life. I remember that I'd had Lucky Charms for breakfast. Lucky Charms!

The taste in my mouth is bitter. My nose is packed with soot, and I'm too short of breath to cough. We're all getting exhausted from inhaling filth. I imagine what the smoke would say if it could talk. *I am going to put all of you to sleep. Heh heh!* I know I am fighting unconsciousness. We all know we are going down. "Lord, You are one. We are three. Have pity on us," Paulo Coelho wrote in *By the River Piedra I Sat and Wept*, one of my favorite novels. I look from

Garrett to Austin, but the smoke is now so thick it swallows us up and as close as they are, I can barely make out their faces. If the fumes don't kill us we will die in the crash. I'd prefer the fumes. I begin to pray. "Lord, have mercy. Christ, have mercy. In the name of the Father, the Son, and the Holy Spirit." I don't even know what that means. I remember hearing it from one of my best friends, Carlos, who is Catholic and gay. He told me it is a universal prayer, the kind you say when you don't know what else to pray. It has been so long since I really prayed, and I'm surprised how easily it comes. "Lord, have mercy. Christ, have mercy. In the name of the Father, the Son, and the Holy Spirit."

I peer out of the window again and see the earth rushing up to meet our falling plane. I can't explain the feeling of powerlessness, of utter fear. If only I can spot a landmark, something so that if I survive the impact I will have my bearings and can try to find help. There is no landmark to see, not a house, or a barn, or a well-traveled road in sight. There is only a spinning blanket of sameness. The plane's engines are screaming, and the noise is deafening. The earth moves closer and closer to our plummeting plane. I brace myself and bury my face deeper into my blouse. I can't bear to see my friends as we crash. Closer. Closer. Closer. Closer. Closer. We are all about to die. Where are You, God?

Garrett!

Austin!

I fight the urge to close my eyes for fear of losing consciousness and the plane hits the ground and skids across fields of crops. I see the tree line just before we slam into it. Boom! I close my eyes, but I can feel things (bodies?) flying and bumping around the cabin. I am constrained by my seatbelt. When I open my eyes again, the plane is mangled and spitting flames. The roof is sheered off, but the blue sky is partially obscured by billowing black smoke. Garrett is to the left of me, hunched forward, too still. Deadly still. I recognize him by his black, collared shirt. I look up and see a body, a human torch, flailing and writhing around the cabin. I can't tell who it is, but I know he is a dead man walking. I feel like I am in some gruesome horror flick. The roar of the spreading fire, coupled with the sickening groan of the engines, drowns out my screams. My lungs beg for air. No mercy. I try unbuckling my seatbelt, but it doesn't budge. I manage to slip out of it, I don't know how.

The door of the plane, what had been the door, behind the left engine, is flapping open, and I crawl over Garrett's body and lunge for the gap. I'm climbing over my lifeless friend, my sweet friend, to save myself. It is already too late for him. The palms of my hands sizzle on a hot metal rod I grab to try to hoist myself out of the plane. I am half in and half out, draped over Garrett's back, but something is stopping me from propelling myself any farther forward. The fire in the plane is spreading. Flames are lashing my legs. If I don't get out now, I will burn to death. I try pulling myself forward again, but I can't budge. What is happening? I look back and see that my legs are crossed and wedged underneath the seatbelt. I am stuck, but I am so weak I can hardly move, and my screams are as good as silence. It dawns on me that I am the only survivor. Everyone else is dead. How can that be? Those boys are all so strong, so much physically and mentally healthier than me. Not only that, I need them. We have so many plans together. I can't bear the thought of my life without them. How easy it would be to just go to sleep. My eyes flutter, and I fight a wave of nausea. I taste death, and it is sweet.

I am about to let myself slip away. My

lungs are betraying me, and my heart feels faint. But then I think about Mom and Papa and Charity and Cameron. What will my family do without me? How will I face my loved ones in the next life if they know how easily I gave up? This is not just my fight. It's about fighting to honor my dead friends. It's about fighting to spare my family and my friends the painful grief of my death. My face strains with determination as I begin to prepare for the battle before me. The battle to live when I know I am dying.

I'm thinking that, by the sheer force of my strong will, I can probably extract one trapped foot from the wreckage. Eventually, the other foot will burn off and, if I live, I will still have one working leg. A burst of adrenaline surges through my body, and I feel a tiny glimmer of hope. I look back to see which foot seems most likely to come free. I am wearing my mother's favorite gray wedges, and the rubber sole on the right shoe is melted, like candle wax, literally fusing my foot to the plastic seat. My left foot has some wiggle room, so I start moving it in tiny, jerking motions. Back and forth. Up and down. After four or five tries, my energy is thoroughly spent, but I decide to make one final attempt to save my life. Using every ounce of force I can muster, I lunge forward, and my left foot comes unstuck. Then, with my newly emancipated left limb as leverage, I push as hard as I can, trying to free my right foot, but it won't budge. Not even a smidgeon. What's left to do? I reach back with my right arm. Maybe I can yank my foot free with my hand? But my arm comes up short, and then the sleeve of my blouse catches fire.

This is a fool's game. I feel as if I'm fighting some unseen opponent who is taunting me, knowing that in the end I am going to die. I seethe with rage. I don't like being played. *I am not going to die like this. You are not going to win.* Using my good foot, I kick so hard I am airborne. Pain sears my groin, my abdomen, my chest. My vision blurs and narrows, and all I can see are darting white stars. I am losing consciousness, I know. *No! I won't pass out. Not now.* I push past Garrett and land on cool grass, a salve for my burning body.

I am out of the plane.

I curl up in a ball on the grass, still within reach of Garrett. I feel too tired to move. My eyes are heavy. I need to rest, just for a minute. I am drifting off to sleep when loud, popping sounds shake me awake. The plane is about to blow us all to smithereens. A battle rages in my head. If I don't move, I will die. But I don't want to leave, not without my friends. The heat radiating from the melting aluminum fuselage is staggering. My will to live wins out, and I stumble to my feet, but my legs feel like jelly, and I crumple to the ground again. My adversary. Jeering. Mocking. *Not so fast,* I say.

I dig my burning hands into the earth and crawl, dragging my limp body behind me, but I'm moving too slowly. If I'm to get away, I have got to get up. I pick up one limb, then the other. This time, my wobbly legs support me, but I look down and see that my clothes, what is left of them, are still smoldering. Stop, drop, and roll. I remembered that from my childhood. I try pulling off what's left of my pants, but I can't tell where the melted black spandex material ends and my blackened, bloody skin begins. The idea of ripping off my own skin makes me gag. I am half-naked. I need to try to make it to people, to civilization, if I am to survive, so I stumble forward, through rows of knee-high corn. No one knows I'm here, wherever I am. My scorched skin is shedding off in sheets, and my lungs feel heavy, as if I'm trying to breathe through mud. There's no way I can make it much longer with all of this damage. I have to live long enough to get help.

I love survival shows. My favorite is *Man Versus Wild,* in which the host, a rugged guy named Bear Grylis, is left stranded in the wild and has to find his way back to civilization. Bear would know what to do. He knows all kinds of survival tricks. What I know is that I need a drink. I am parched and choking on the junk clogging my nose and throat. Bear would dig beneath the plants for water, but that will take too long, and I don't have enough strength for digging anyway. Panic sets in. My breathing is fast and shallow, and my heart is skipping wildly. *Calm down, Hannah. Panicking will only make things worse.* I hear an explosion, and I fall to my knees. Holding my face in my hands, I think I scream, but my voice is barely a whisper. "Help me! Please! Is there anybody there?" I don't know where to turn, what to do, and I look back at the plane. That's when I see him.

At first I think it is a stranger, some random person who was hit by our crashing airplane. What are the chances of that? I know I'm thinking crazy. He has emerged from behind a tree and is standing near the fiery plane, brushing himself off. I call out to him. "Hello? Who are you? I need help!" As he walks toward me, I realize this is no stranger. I would know Austin's cocky soldier's stride anywhere. He marches toward me and stops when our noses are just inches apart. He is covered in blood, his hair is burned off, and a slice of the right side of his head is gone. Except for his dress shoes and a piece of one sock melted into his leg, he is naked. In a desperate act of modesty, he holds his hand over his genitals. I have never seen Austin so vulnerable, and I choke back sobs.

"Austin?" I cry. "Austin? Is that you?"

"Yeah, dummy, it's me," he says.

Austin, my wonderful friend. Somehow, he is calm, and that calms me. I want to hug him, but I'm afraid of hurting him.

"Hannah!" he says, staring into my eyes, his manner deadly serious. "I want you to tell me the truth. Do I look okay?"

"Yes, yes Austin!" I lie. "You look fine. Do I look okay?"

"Yeah" he says. "You look fine."

We both smile and, for that brief moment, we are just two vain college kids reassuring each other about their looks.

"Now, c'mon," he says. "Let's go."

Austin takes off walking. I know he is afraid, but he is determined and completely in command of himself. I am willing to follow him anywhere. Not only is he the most

227

trustworthy person I know, he is a Marine, trained for war, and we are in a fight for our lives. As we make our way through the field of waist-high corn, the coarse stalks gouge my raw, bleeding burns. We are acting on pure adrenaline. And Austin is in worse shape than me. I know he needs water and, at this point, I would drink sewer water to wet my parched throat. "Austin!" I cry out. "Eat grass! Eat grass!" But he keeps walking. I follow along, trying to keep up with his swift pace. Finally, we reach a hedgerow and beyond that a gravel road. I look both ways. The road looks endless, a road to nowhere. I can't imagine it is very well traveled. I begin to lose hope. If we don't find help, and soon, we will die out here in this no-man's-land.

My mind is going to the darkest of places when, suddenly, I am roused by the sound of tires crunching on gravel. Austin sees the minivan before I do. At first, I wonder if it is an illusion. "C'mon," he says, all business, heading up the road toward the oncoming car. I know we look like a couple of zombies out of *The Walking Dead*. The closer the car comes, the slower it moves. Stop. Go. Stop. Go. I wave my arms. Are they afraid of us? "Help us!" I cry. "Please, we need help!" The car stops a few feet away, and we continue walking, stumbling, toward it. I can see two women inside. *My God, I think. We're going to be saved.*

Just then, the driver shifts the car into reverse. Our saviors are backing away. *What are they doing? What in God's name are they doing?*

## LINDA'S STORY

My friend Heather had been going through a lot in her life. She'd been diagnosed with MS, which would be a blow for anyone, but especially someone so young and energetic. One day, thinking about how fragile life is, she wrote a list of things she wanted to accomplish, her bucket list. One of the items on the list was shooting a gun, something she had never done. My husband is a hunter, and I was on the rifle team in college, so we offered to teach her.

That's where we were going that afternoon, to meet my husband after work at a private shooting range in Fredonia, a thirty-minute drive from where we live in Chanute.

## HEATHER'S STORY

I almost cancelled our trip. I take a shot once a week for MS, and that day I had trouble injecting myself. The shots hurt, but it's the cost of the fight, so you work past the pain. That day was different, though. I'm not sure what I did — maybe I hit a nerve, or the bone — but whatever it was, it felt like a red-hot poker searing through my arm when I injected myself. I pulled the needle out, dropped onto my bed, and sobbed. For the next few minutes, I debated whether to just stay there. But as the pain began to ease, I decided that getting out might help take my mind off my aching arm.

When I heard Linda pull into the driveway, I went to the bathroom to wash my face with cold water. My eyes were red and swollen from crying. I hoped Linda wouldn't notice. I didn't want to have to explain. Before heading out the door, I grabbed my sunglasses, some Tylenol, and a bottle of water from the refrigerator. I glanced at my watch. We were running about seven minutes behind. We would have to hurry to make our appointment.

## LINDA'S STORY

When we finally got going, I headed for the shortcut on the county road rather than take the highway to Fredonia.

We were about halfway there when both Heather and I noticed a plume of smoke on the horizon. She wasn't familiar with that territory, but I travel the rural route quite often, and it's not unusual to see small brush fires, or someone burning their harvested field. This smoke looked different, though. It was shaped like a mushroom. Heather said she thought that mushroom clouds formed from explosions. I knew there were oil and gas wells in that area, but I still wasn't overly concerned. "But let's go see," I said. I headed in the direction of the smoke, which led us off the main route to a gravel road I'd never driven before. As soon as we hit the gravel, and the dust kicked up, Heather muttered something about turning around. "No sense getting the car all dirty for nothing," she said.

I guess my curiosity got the best of me because I stayed the course.

## HEATHER'S STORY
We had probably gone a mile or so on the gravel road and we were getting closer to the smoke when, all of a sudden, we saw two people step out onto the road. We were still far enough away that it was hard to make out exactly what we were seeing. One person was wearing black. The other, a nude or tan color, or so we thought. It was odd seeing people there. My friend Linda stopped the car and looked at me as if to

231

say, "What is this?" Honestly, at that point, things weren't registering. We were encountering something we weren't expecting, something we'd never seen before, and we didn't know what to make of it. We had no frame of reference. A little bit of self-preservation kicked in, and I was thinking to myself, "I don't know what this is, and I don't know that I want to be here." I knew my friend was having the same thoughts.

I had my phone in my hand by then. "I'm going to call 911," I said. I had just begun describing to the operator what we were seeing. "Two people . . . Something's really wrong . . . I don't know what happened but you need to send someone . . ." She asked what county we were in. I had no idea, so I handed the phone to Linda so she could explain where we were and, just as I did, I saw the two people coming closer to us. Linda put the car in reverse and started backing up, to put space between us and the forbidding scene playing out. She had backed up only a few inches when the girl put her hand in the air and said something.

"Water!" she cried. "Please! We need water!" She and her companion walked closer to the car, and I could see then they were in no condition to attack us. She was bleeding, and her clothes were ripped and

232

smoldering. He was naked and trying to cover himself. They were not trying to get something from us — to rob us or to hurt us. Something terrible had happened to them, and they needed our help.

I grabbed my bottle of water and swung open the car door.

"What are you doing?" my friend asked.

"I'm giving them water," I said, stepping out of the minivan and shutting the door behind me.

Austin and I were so relieved when the minivan stopped again and the young woman got out. She looked only a few years older than me. I could see the fear in her eyes as she walked toward Austin and me, holding a bottle of water in her hand.

"What happened?" she asked.

"A plane crash," Austin choked out.

"Are there others?"

"Three others," he said. "I don't think they made it."

She said her name was Heather, and she uncapped the bottle of water and handed it to Austin. He pointed to me. "Her first," he said. I guzzled about half the bottle, then she handed him the rest. He tipped the bottle to his lips and drank, but, after a moment, the water dribbled out of his mouth.

He tried again and the same thing happened. Austin couldn't swallow.

Heather told us she had called 911 and promised that help was on the way. "Can't you just take us to a hospital?" I asked. It was all I could do to get a breath, my lungs just weren't working right, but Heather said we needed to stay put and wait for the EMTs to arrive. I was frustrated and scared. I sat in the brush by the side of the road, while Heather stood with Austin, asking him questions.

"Who was in the plane?" she asked.

"Five of us," he said, and proceeded to give her all of our names. "We came from Tulsa. We were on our way to an event in Council Bluffs."

She asked Austin if he wanted to sit down, too, but he said he couldn't. He looked gravely injured, yet he was completely calm and in control. He answered every question posed to him and even asked some of his own.

## HEATHER'S STORY

He said, "I look bad, don't I?" And I said, "Well, I don't know. It looks like you have burns and a nice gash on your head that you can show off to all of your friends, but I think you'll be just fine." I ran back to the car to find something to cover him. My friend Linda had a basket of clean laundry, so I grabbed a sheet from it and held it in front of him because his hands were too damaged to hold it himself. I wanted him to have his dignity. A minute or two later, he asked me again. "How bad is it?" He stepped closer to me when he said it this time. I think he really wanted to know. So I said, "Well, it's not good, Austin, but I think you'll make it just fine." He didn't ask me again after that. He was concerned about Hannah. He wanted to make sure that she had enough water, and that she wasn't in too much pain and was going to be okay. Hannah kept saying she couldn't breathe. It killed me because there was nothing I could do. All I could say was, "Honey, I can't help. I'm so sorry. We just have to wait for the ambulance to arrive." Without thinking, I put my hand on her shoulder, and she screamed. "I'm so sorry," I said. "What can I do?" Hannah looked me in the eye. "Please just pray for us," she pleaded. I put my hand over her and started praying and, when I did, Austin stepped closer, and we all prayed together.

I got off the phone from the 911 call, confident that the rescue workers knew how to find us, and I walked over to where Heather was standing with Austin and Hannah. Heather was standing closest to Austin, asking him a series of questions to keep him from falling into unconsciousness, and Hannah was sitting on the side of the road. I noticed that her hair was singed and her clothes, what was left of them, were disheveled. She begged me to pull off her pants because they were burning her legs. My heart ached, knowing there was no way I could pull them off . . . they were melted into her skin.

She asked if I would call her father to tell him what had happened. I pulled out my phone and punched in the numbers she recited, thinking, "I don't know what to say to this man." When he answered I choked out something like, "I'm with your daughter, Hannah. There's been an accident but she's all right." He asked, "What do you mean? My daughter's on a plane. Where's the plane?" I told him the plane was off in the distance, and it was on fire. I said "She's standing here with a young man." He asked his name. "His name is Austin," I said. "Where are the others?" he asked. "There are no others," I said.

## HEATHER'S STORY

It was taking forever for help to arrive, or at least it seemed that way. I had asked Austin the same questions over and over, and I could tell he was getting irritated. What's your brother's name? *Aubrey.* How many siblings do you have? *Two.* What are their ages? *Allie, sixteen. Aubrey, twenty-four.* What's your mom's name? *Mary.* How about your father? *Monte, deceased.* I don't remember whether he rolled his eyes, or if he even could roll his eyes, but somehow he expressed to me that he was getting annoyed at having to answer the same questions so many times. I could tell how much pain he was in. With the slightest breeze, he shifted from side to side, looking for a way to block the wind from brushing against his seared skin. Who should I contact for you? I asked. "My grandpa," he said, reciting his grandfather's phone number. Even with that kind of suffering, Austin had the presence of mind to answer everything I asked, and even remember the phone number. I found myself overcome with feelings of awe and admiration for him.

I was so worried about Austin. The ambulance still wasn't coming, and he was getting worse. He couldn't move his arms or legs, and he wasn't talking nearly as much. I saw such determination in his eyes. He had so much courage. I kept thinking, if he can be resilient, so can I. He was in so much pain. I hated seeing him that way. I was still sitting and I felt this terrible burning sensation on my backside. I shot upright, and when I did I saw Linda getting back into the minivan. I thought she and Heather were going to leave us there, in the godforsaken field, and I panicked. "Where's she going?" I cried. Heather assured me that Linda wasn't going far. She wanted to check a nearby road sign to make sure she had given the 911 operator the proper crossroad. I guess it was the child inside me, but I still felt abandoned. Didn't she see how Austin and I were suffering?

As I was thinking my irrational thoughts, I looked down at my body. "What's crawling on me?" I screamed. "Get them off of me!" Growing up in rural Texas, I knew the feeling of being stung by fire ants. Now they were crawling all over my body. "Get them off of me!" I screamed again. Heather looked at me as if I had lost my mind. "Honey," she said, clearly perplexed but reassuringly. "Honey, there's nothing on you."

I calmed down for a moment. Maybe it's the wind I feel, I thought. I shuddered. My body felt as if it was being eaten alive. "Dear God!" I cried. "Get me out of this damned body!"

Up until then, I had been trying really hard to hold on for both Austin and me, but I started feeling as if I was going to black out. I was afraid that then I would go into shock and die. I thought I remembered Heather saying she worked with kindergartners, so I asked her to tell me a story. I said I needed to stay focused on something so I didn't lose consciousness. "Look, I need you to help me to keep my eyes open so I don't go into shock." I'd start to fade away and I'd hear her shouting "HANNAII! HANNAH!"

"Tell me a fairytale," I pleaded. Heather said she didn't know many stories. "Tell me the story of Peter Pan." I could tell she was trying, but she didn't even remember that the Lost Boys had encounters with pirates and fairies. I was finding it harder and harder to stay aware. "Talk to me!" I pleaded. "Ask me questions! Anything." She started telling me about her kindergartners, but I drifted off. She wasn't a very good storyteller.

Hannah started having more trouble. She stood up in the road, pleading with me to talk to her and tell her stories. Suddenly I remembered a story we had read in class a while back. It was a beautiful little story called "The Empty Pot," in which the Chinese emperor proclaims that his successor to the throne will be the child who can grow the most beautiful flowers from seeds. *"A long time ago in China there was a boy named Ping who loved flowers. Anything he planted burst into bloom. Up came flowers, bushes, and even big fruit trees, as if by magic . . ."* Hannah's eyes seared into mine. I could tell she was struggling to stay with me, struggling to maintain lucidity. Fighting not to die. Her body was shutting down. Her knees would buckle, and her face would tighten up, but then she would squeeze her eyes closed and stand up again. It happened over and over again. Her eyes would roll back and she would blink really hard and stare into my eyes, as if to say, "I AM NOT GOING ANYWHERE!" I could see the determination on her face, and it was intense. Her will was forcing her body to do what she wanted it to do. I have never seen anything like it in my life.

# 22
## RESCUE

When I am afraid, I put my trust in you.
— PSALM 56:3

I heard the distant bray of sirens, signaling that help was finally on the way. The first ambulance kicked up dust on the gravel road as it sped toward us. I can't even describe my relief. Only a moment earlier, I was mustering my last bit of strength to stay conscious because I was certain I was going to die. *Finally*, I thought, stumbling toward the approaching ambulance, its lights flashing and its sirens screaming. *Finally*, I thought. *Finally I can let go.* But before I gave in to the darkness, I wanted to be sure that Austin was going to be okay.

The ambulance roared to a stop, and two paramedics jumped out. Just then, the first of a parade of fire trucks and police cars began arriving. Heather asked the rescue workers for more water for us and she was able to scrounge up four bottles and split them between Austin and me. I guzzled mine. Austin tried to, but he still couldn't get the liquid down. Once again, it dribbled out of his mouth and down his chin. "Please, God, let him live," I prayed.

I could tell from the faces of some of the firemen that they had never seen anything so gruesome as how Austin and I looked. Our exposed bodies were oozing blood and gore, and our burned skin was shedding off in sheets, leaving piles of clotted gray ash at our feet. They tried not to stare, but I could see from their expressions of shock — or was it revulsion — that we were a sight. I know on a few of their faces I saw fear, perhaps reflecting the terror in my own eyes.

The paramedics took Austin first into the ambulance. He couldn't move, and they had to lay him on a gurney and carry him. He was a big, powerful boy, and I heard a lot of grunts and groans as they struggled to get him up into the rig. By the time I got there they were already working on him. I could hear one of the paramedics talking to him, while the others ushered me to the back of the ambulance. I was anxious to get inside to try to talk with him, but I couldn't step up because what was left of my pants, the parts that hadn't melted into my legs, was down around my ankles, binding them together like a thick rope. When one of the emergency workers tried to help me step up to get inside, I screamed and nearly blacked out. I heard someone shout, "Be careful with her! Be careful with her!" After that, a couple of them lifted me up and into the ambulance and put me on a sideboard next to Austin. I wished I had been able to hold his hand.

I begged the paramedics to cut off what was left of my clothes. I remember thinking that I was glad my pretty blouse had been spared because it belonged to my mom and was one of her favorites. Of course, I must have been confused, because my back and right arm were scorched, so there was no way the blouse had survived. A female EMT stripped off my clothes, but my socks and shoes were melted to my feet, and they were still burning me. "Please!" I cried. "Please get them off!" I felt for my necklace, a crystal heart with the word LOVE written across it. As I did, I noticed the smell of my own burning hair, and I felt the top of my head, trying to gauge what was left of it and whether it was still on fire. When I touched my head, clumps of my chestnut hair fell off onto the pillow. I quickly pulled back my hand. "Okay," I told myself. "I can't touch my head again or all of it will fall off and I won't have any hair left."

"Austin," I whispered.

"Austin? Are you okay?"

## Fire Chief Duane Banzet's Story

Our department was dispatched to an airplane crash in rural Altoona, Kansas. We responded with an ambulance and two fire trucks. I also requested mutual aid from the Chanute Fire Department, Neosho Memorial Regional Medical Center Emergency Medical Services, Fredonia Regional Medical Center Emergency Medical Services, and an Eagle medical helicopter.

A Kansas Wildlife and Parks game warden officer, Bob Funky, was just a few miles away when the 911 call came in. He was the first to arrive on the scene and he found Austin and Hannah, both of them badly burned and nearly naked, standing alongside the road with the two women who called in the emergency. The women were holding a sheet in front of them to shield their nakedness.

Officer Funky then drove through the cornfield to the burning plane. There, he discovered the bodies of the other three. Garrett and Luke were still inside the plane.

Stephen's body was outside, near the port-side wing. He was less burned than the others.

I got to the field just as Hannah and Austin were walking to an ambulance. In my twenty-five years in this line of work, I have never seen anyone who was burned as badly as Austin and still alive, let alone able to walk. The only part of his body that appeared to be spared was his eyes. I prayed to God. "Please help us."

### HEATHER'S STORY

Once Austin and Hannah were finally in the ambulance, one of the paramedics, a woman, called to me to "Get in here!" I jumped up into the truck, and she motioned for me to sit between Austin and Hannah. She gave me a clipboard and told me to start writing their answers to the questions she was asking.

*"Names?"*

"Austin Anderson."

"Hannah Luce."

*"Do you have any allergies?"*

"None."

"No."

*"Who do you want us to call?"*

"My grandpa," Austin said, again reciting the phone number in Oklahoma.

Hannah was nodding off. She was having a lot of trouble staying with us at that point. I really thought we were losing her. "Hannah!" I said. "Think about your sister and brother. Think about how happy they will be when they know you're okay."

The paramedics took over, and I turned my full attention to Austin. It could only have been by the grace of God that he was still lucid. "I can't move," he said.

"Stay with me, Austin," I said. "Are you with me?" He tipped his head forward a bit. "Yes," he said.

What happened next is still so hard to talk about. I heard the paramedics saying they would have to do a procedure on both Austin and Hannah called intraosseous infusion, in which they drill an IV line through bone to the marrow to administer the necessary fluids to prevent shock. They had to go that route because they couldn't use a standard intravenous line with such serious burns. I watched in horror as the paramedic pulled out a long, spring-loaded needle and drove it into Austin's knee. His body jerked, and he screamed out in pain. "What are you doing?" he asked. "Giving you medicine," the medic said. "It doesn't feel like medicine," Austin replied. Then it was Hannah's turn. She, too, screamed, and when it was over, she tearfully looked into the medic's eyes and asked him if he would hold her hand, which he did. "Can I let go now?" she asked. She had been fighting unconsciousness for so long, and she wanted permission to let her body take over. "Yes, you can let go now," he said.

I could hardly believe it when they said that they had to inject Austin again. The first time hadn't worked. I had to look away, but I heard him curse the paramedic, and I knew when it was over because Austin bolted upright and started pulling at his shoes. He wanted out of there. The medics tried to calm Austin, and they began asking him questions to keep him from going into shock before the medication had a chance to work. "What happened out there?" one of them asked.

"A plane crash," Austin said, clearly agitated.

"Where was the plane headed?"

"Council Bluffs," Austin answered.

"What's in Council Bluffs?"

"Acquire the Fire," Austin said.

My mouth dropped. "What did you say?" I asked. "Did you say Acquire the Fire?"

Austin nodded. "Yes."

That's when it really hit me, the significance of the situation. At least in Christian circles, everyone knows about the Teen Mania ministry and their Acquire the Fire Christian youth rallies. Teenagers from our area attended them when they were nearby. These were serious Christian kids I was with. I looked from one to the other and thought, "You ran into two Christian women who have been praying their guts out from the moment we met you. God knows what's going on here. He knew about this before we did, and that's why He put us here. I don't understand why this happened, but He hasn't abandoned us. He's right here."

As I silently marveled about my revelation, Hannah was taken to a second ambulance that had arrived. I said good-bye and told her I would be praying for her. We were waiting for a helicopter that was to airlift Austin to a trauma center in Wichita. I was sitting on the bench, next to his head, praying with him, when one of the medics said Austin needed to be intubated, and I probably didn't want to watch. I knew that meant forcing a breathing tube down his throat, and I was thankful for the warning.

Austin couldn't talk anymore after that. The paramedic said he was fighting the pain medication, fighting to stay awake. The medic seemed awed by Austin's grit. I know I was.

"Austin," I said, leaning in close. "You're in good hands. God is with you. He has never left your side." I was looking into his eyes and he was looking into mine. "God's got you," I said. "You can relax."

His body relaxed, and I could tell he had let go. He closed his eyes. He wasn't fighting anymore.

# 23
## SOLE SURVIVOR

So now faith, hope, and love abide, these three; but the greatest of these is love.
— 1 CORINTHIANS 13:13

KANSAS CITY, Mo. (AP) — A small airplane that crashed in southeast Kansas was carrying five people with connections to Oral Roberts University to a Christian youth rally in Iowa, a friend of three of the victims said Saturday.

The Kansas Highway Patrol reported that four of the passengers died in Friday's crash and one was badly injured. Those killed were identified Saturday as pilot Luke Sheets, 23, of Ephraim, Wis.; Austin Anderson, 27, of Ringwood, Okla.; Garrett Coble, 29, of Tulsa, Okla.; and Stephen Luth, 22, of Muscatine, Iowa.

Hannah Luce, 22, of Garden Valley, Texas, was critically injured and admitted to the University of Kansas Medical Center in Kansas City, Kan. Luce, a recent Oral Roberts graduate, is the daughter of Ron Luce, a trustee at the school and the founder of Teen Mania Ministries, which was sponsoring this weekend's Acquire the Fire rally in Council Bluff, Iowa.

The National Transportation Safety Board said the twin-engine Cessna 401 went down around 4:30 p.m. Friday northwest of Chanute, Kan. NTSB spokesman Peter Knudson said the eight-seat plane caught fire after the crash.

"The plane lost contact with air traffic control after getting permission to descend to a lower altitude," Knudson said. "After that, there was no further communication."

## KATIE'S STORY

I got a call from my husband late in the afternoon. He sounded grave, and his words were slow and calculated, which scared me. He said, "Honey, I have something very serious to tell you — Hannah's okay, but the plane went down. She and Austin got out, but we don't know about the other boys." My head was spinning. Wait. What? The plane went down? My mind raced back to the day, twenty-one years earlier, when I received a similar call from a friend who'd said Ron's plane had gone down, but he and the three others who were on board had all survived. How uncanny that the same thing had just happened to our daughter. I was trying to wrap my mind around all of it, when I heard Ron say that the lady who found Hannah and Austin on the side of the road had called him and put Hannah on the phone, but she'd spoken only a word or two. Ron said she'd sounded as if she was in shock.

We had to get a flight to Kansas as soon as possible. I threw four shirts into a bag, thinking that would probably be too much for the trip, and we jumped into the car and headed for the airport, not even knowing where we were going once we got to Kansas. Ron kept calling Heather, the woman who found Hannah. She gave him a phone number for a police officer who was on site. It was the officer who told us Garrett, Stephen, and Luke hadn't made it. What a nightmare the day was. All we could do was weep.

We finally learned that Austin and Hannah had been taken to two different hospitals. Hannah was in Kansas City. Our friend Lou picked us up from the airport and drove us straight there. He is known for his strong prayer life, and that's exactly what we needed at that moment. His wife brought me a pillow and a blanket. (Little did I know I'd be using them on a couch in the waiting room for weeks to come.)

When we finally saw Hannah, our hearts broke into a thousand pieces. She was swollen and unable to speak. Her anxious gaze met our desperate faces, and all I wanted to do was run to her, hold her, and make this nightmare go away.

## RON'S STORY

Katie and I were shocked when we walked into the hospital room. That wasn't our daughter lying there. It didn't look anything like Hannah. Her body was swollen to nearly twice its size, and she was hooked up to a snarl of tubes and wires. A plastic tube protruded from her mouth, and a machine was breathing for her. I just remember the beep, beep, beep of the machines. I didn't think she was lucid, but apparently she was. Our eyes must have told a story because when she looked at us she got a look of terror on her face. She seemed to try to say something, but the intubation tube in her trachea prevented her from speaking, and she drifted in and out of consciousness after that. Looking at her, I thought it was a miracle that she was still alive.

The doctors told us it would be touch and

go those first few hours and maybe even for the first few days while they assessed her burns and the damage to her lungs. I felt so helpless. There was nothing we could do to help her. I spent the night praying by her bedside. Praying thanks that Hannah's life had been spared and praying for the families who were grieving their children.

"Thank you, Jesus, for your protection for Hannah. We don't understand this at all. Why were the others not protected? How can we rejoice when the others suffer loss? Help us to be good parents to Hannah through all of this. We need your grace now more than ever before."

Those first twenty-four hours were a blur. People from all over were calling and messaging. I was taking calls from every major media outlet. Everyone wanted the story. *Good Morning America. The Today Show.* The Associated Press. Fox. CNN. People from all over the country and around the world were sending prayers and asking what happened. What could we tell them? The only person who knew was our girl, and she couldn't speak.

The first person I saw when I woke up was Papa. He looked so sad and so tired. I had been sleeping for a day or two, and he was camped out on a chair next to my bed. He never left my side. When I woke up, he was holding my hand.

My body felt like it was on fire. I had never experienced such excruciating pain. I pointed to the breathing tube. I wanted it out, but Papa told me that I had smoke damage and one of my lungs had collapsed. I felt so helpless and afraid. I was hooked up to all of these tubes and machines, and I couldn't move anything. Parts of my body were covered in gauze, and it felt like a chunk was missing from my lip. I had questions, so many questions, but no way to ask them. I was trying to speak and making gurgling sounds, and Papa was trying to calm me down. A nurse brought me a piece of paper and a pencil. My right hand was bandaged, so I had to use my left hand to write. "How is everyone else?" I wrote. "How is Austin?"

## RON'S STORY

Every once in a while during those first couple of days she would write notes. It was chicken scratch, but we usually managed to figure out what she was trying to tell us. She brought it up three or four times. "How is everybody? How is Austin?" We didn't want to tell her so soon, so we'd change the subject or pretend to be tending to something else. She was going through so much physically we didn't want to put even more stress on her. But on Day Three she wrote one word: "Austin," followed by a big question mark. I looked into her eyes, and I knew she wouldn't be deterred from getting her answer. She held my eyes and wouldn't look away. The look in her eyes was one of fierce resolve.

"Austin?" My eyes teared up, and I grabbed her hand and shook my head slowly from side to side. Austin had survived only a few hours after the crash. He'd been burned over 90 percent of his body. He never had a chance. It was a miracle that he survived as long as he did, but he held on until his family and his fiancée, Elizabeth, could get there.

Hannah began to sob uncontrollably.

# 24
# THE MEDIA

He did what heroes do after their work is accomplished; he died.
— LEO TOLSTOY, *WAR AND PEACE*

## RON'S STORY

On Sunday, two days after the crash, I held a press conference in the lobby of the University of Kansas Hospital in Kansas City. Hannah was still in the burn intensive care unit three floors up, and she was a very sick girl. She was in tough shape, having suffered third-degree burns over the whole right side of her body, as well as her bottom, and her lungs were singed. But Hannah was a fighter. The doctors said they were stunned she hadn't suffered internal or brain injuries or broken any bones in the crash. She was in critical but stable condition and, barring a life-threatening infection, which was always a possibility with burn patients, her chances for survival were encouraging. The doctors were fantastic. They were trying to provide us with hope, yet at the same time we were well aware of the seriousness of her injuries. A man in the bed next to her had less severe burns but died from the kind of infection the doctors had warned us about. Katie and I were in her room every minute, watching everything the medical team did, and questioning all of it. Hannah had survived the plane crash with a miracle. There was no way I was going to let a distracted nurse or technician push a wrong button or inject the wrong medicine.

For two days, the media had been waiting outside the hospital for some word on Hannah's condition. All of the major stations were there, as well as the local media. We'd been following the news stories in the newspapers and on TV. All of the reports said Austin pulled Hannah from the plane. All of the papers had headlines about the hero Marine who'd saved our Hannah's life.

From national news channels to newspaper headlines, everyone took the hero angle. "Former Marine Dies Saving Friend From Plane Crash," one said. "A Final Act of Valor," another said. The *New York Daily News* wrote, "Austin Anderson, a 27-year-old former Marine who had served two tours in Iraq, suffered burns over 90% of his body in the crash but managed to pull Luce from the wreckage, authorities said. The pair then walked to a nearby road for help."

Katie and I couldn't find anyone "official" to substantiate the story. The news reports didn't quote authorities, only a couple of kids from ORU. One girl, who said she was a friend of Austin's, told a reporter, "[Austin] got out, but he went to get Hannah as well, and that's how his lungs got burned." Another girl, who identified herself as a friend from ORU as well, told a TV station the same story, that Austin had pulled Hannah from the fiery plane, sacrificing his own life. When the reporter asked how she knew, the girl said that Hannah had written it on a piece of paper to us in the hospital. Katie and I knew that wasn't true. Hannah hadn't written anything about Austin other than her brief note with his name and a question mark.

I knew that Austin's role in saving Hannah would be a major focus at the news conference, and I wasn't sure how I'd handle it because I really didn't know at that point what the truth was. Hannah was the only person alive who knew what happened, and she hadn't told us anything about the crash.

I went downstairs to face an onslaught of reporters and gave them an update on Hannah's condition. I said that while she was still in serious condition, burned over nearly 30 percent of her body and in a tremendous amount of pain, we were cautiously optimistic about her recovery. I told them she was scheduled for her first skin graft surgery the following morning.

One of the reporters asked how I found out about the crash. I answered, "The way I discovered about my daughter and the plane accident was probably the most unscripted way you could imagine. One of the women who found Hannah and Austin after the crash called me. I asked her, 'Where's the plane?' And she said, 'It's off in the distance, and there are flames, there's smoke.' "

Someone else asked what I knew about the boys on the plane. I told them that all four were extraordinary young men who were committed to their Christian faith. "There could be no prouder parents than the parents of the four remarkable young men who were killed," I said.

Then, the inevitable question was asked. What did I think about the young Marine, Austin Anderson, the hero who had given his life to save my firstborn?

I took a deep breath and shook my head. I said that we'd asked Hannah about the reports we'd heard about Austin saving her, and she'd teared up but hadn't been able to answer. Then I said, "I know Austin, he's that kind of guy. He served two tours in Iraq, and he was willing to give his life for his country. He was willing to give his life for a friend. He was always willing to go that extra mile."

I knew that much was true.

# 25
## FIRST WORDS

Is any sick among you? Let him call for the elders of the church; and let them pray over him, anointing him with oil in the name of the Lord.

— JAMES 5:14

### RON'S STORY

Katie and I were swamped with phone calls and messages from well-wishers that first weekend. Churches around the world were praying for Hannah's recovery. On Monday, we wrote our first dispatch from the hospital. The doctors had reassured us by then that Hannah had a long way to go to heal, but she was no longer in a life-threatening situation and had been downgraded to serious but stable condition. Here's what we wrote:

Dear Family and Friends,
    As you may have seen or heard in the

news media over the weekend, this last Friday afternoon a small plane carrying five passengers crashed in rural southeastern Kansas en route to an Acquire the Fire event in Council Bluffs, Iowa. So it is with a heavy heart that I stop for a moment to write this quick note — to update you on the situation and ask for your prayers.

As you would expect, the last couple of days have been a blur of shock and sadness and concern. But I know that reports of this tragedy have been all over the news and that as a friend of this ministry you would be profoundly concerned. So I wanted to get a quick note to you now to share our hearts and to help you know how to pray in the days ahead.

There is much we don't yet know. But we do know that when the plane went down, three of the five on board died at the scene. These were (pilot) Luke Sheets, Garrett Coble, and Stephen Luth. Hannah and the fifth passenger, Austin Anderson, a Marine who had served two tours of duty in Iraq, were able to escape from the burning plane and walk to a nearby roadway to get help.

However, both Hannah and Austin suffered severe injuries and were life-flighted to hospitals in Kansas City and Wichita, respectively. Hannah was listed in serious but stable condition, suffering primarily from burns on 28% of her body. Austin's burn injuries were far more severe, especially those sustained to his lungs. At about 5:30 a.m. Saturday, Austin went to be with the Lord.

We believe he helped Hannah out of the plane and to the roadside. Not only is he a hero for serving our nation, we probably owe our daughter's life to his courage and strength.

Of course, the entire Teen Mania family is mourning the loss of these four young lives. They were so full of promise and love for God. All were friends of Teen Mania, and two of them, Austin and Stephen, were only recently hired to join our marketing team. Katie and I will share additional updates as we can. For now I would ask that you help us by lifting some very specific needs to the Father in prayer.

Right now our most intense concern is for the families of those who died. Please pray that God surrounds the families of Austin, Stephen, Luke, and Garrett with

His supernatural love and peace in this tremendously difficult time.

Also, as the Lord leads, please pray for a quick and supernatural recovery for our Hannah. As of today, the update on her condition is one of improvement. She is recovering well at a hospital in Kansas City. This morning, the doctors took her off the ventilator and she is breathing on her own. They have removed the tube from her throat so that she will be able to speak. She is growing stronger, more coherent, and is asking questions. The burning and soot in her lungs has been suctioned out and is healing up. The doctors are reporting the damage will not be long-term.

It is truly a miracle that she is alive. Grief counselors will be seeing Hannah throughout the next few weeks, as her heart is heavy with the grief for the loss of her friends. She will be beginning skin graft surgeries right away for the third-degree burns she sustained on the back of her hands and her lower left leg.

Please hold us up in prayer. If you have friends or loved ones whom you know to be effective intercessors, please feel free to forward this message to them with an encouragement to lift us up.

Still Consumed, Ron and Katie

My hands were tied to the bed rails, and I felt as if red-hot coals were burning my bottom. It was Day Three of the new Hannah Nicole Luce, a girl who had once lived a pretty privileged life but was now deep in some hellish nightmare. The last thing I knew I was on a gurney in an electric blue operating room being prepped for skin graft surgery, the first of several I was scheduled to have. (The doctor had said he wanted to start grafting right away, before my skin began healing.) The anesthesiologist was saying something about counting backward from ten, and all I could think was my friends were dead and all of the anesthesia in the world wouldn't blunt that pain.

When I got back to my hospital room, it didn't look like my hospital room. The color of the furniture was wrong, green not tan, the sequence of pictures on the wall was different, and I didn't have a white board with a nurse's name written on it before. I blinked, thinking that maybe when I opened my eyes again I'd recognize the room, but nothing changed. Where was I?

My skin throbbed with a kind of pain I couldn't have imagined before and can't begin to describe. I couldn't get my limbs to move, and my right leg was suspended in the air. The worst part was having my hands bound to the bed. I didn't know why someone would do that to me. I was trapped in my own body, unable to talk or move, and I was terrified. At least before I could use my good hand to write a question or a thought, but now the only way I would be able to communicate was with my eyes, but first I had to get someone's attention.

Mom was there somewhere close by. I could hear her talking with one of the nurses. I moved my eyes to the right and saw them standing there, on the side of my bed. How will Mom know I'm awake? I wondered. What if she leaves me here like this? Panic welled up inside me. I wiggled a finger on my left hand, the one that wasn't wrapped up in a gauze mitt. It took all of my strength to do it again, then again. I heard a lull in the conversation. Thank You, God. The nurse walked closer to my bed and leaned over me.

I opened my eyes as wide as I could so she'd know I was in there. I tapped my left finger to reiterate my point: *"I'm awake!"* When I knew I had her attention, I moved my eyes dramatically from left to right. *"Get these restraints off!"* The nurse was maddeningly casual. "Oh, well, she's just trying to get out of her restraints," she said, coolly. I hated her at that moment. "Oh, well," I thought. "When I do get out of these handcuffs I'm going to crack you in the nose."

I tapped my finger wildly (as wildly as you can tap one finger), and Mom moved closer. My mother is the sweetest person in the world. She oozes kindness and compassion, and I could see the hurt and concern in her eyes. She explained that I'd been moved to a different room after surgery, a bigger, prettier room with a nice view! My eyes drilled into her eyes. I looked down at the restraints and back at her. *Get them off!"*

She touched my head and gently explained that my hands were tied down because I'd been trying to pull out my breathing tube. I understood that would have been ugly because the tube went down my throat, past my vocal cords, and into the airways of my lungs. But I was gagging on that tube. I'm not sure which was worse, gagging or being tied down. I held Mom's eyes, pleading now. *"Please, Mom. Please help me."*

Mom turned to the nurse, "Please," she said. "Take them off."

When my hands were finally free I motioned that I wanted to write something. Mom brought me a piece of paper and a pen. "I love you," I wrote. She decided to speak in my language by writing her response. "I ADORE THE GROUND YOU WALK ON!" she wrote back.

The next time I woke up, it was the following morning, and Mom wasn't with me. I was lying on a steel table in the middle of a tile room with no windows and a ceiling so low I felt as if I could touch it — if I'd been able to raise my arm. The room was hot and steamy, like a sauna, and it smelled musty and stale. As I lay there, drugged and wondering if I was dreaming, a black hose dropped from the ceiling. A team of masked strangers descended on me, five of them, all dressed in green scrubs and wearing strange-looking purple gloves. "Is this a gas chamber?" I wondered.

No, but it was what I would come to think of as a torture chamber. I was in the hydrotherapy or "tank room," the place where burn patients are taken every day to have their wounds cleansed. The skin is the first line of defense against infections, and burned skin isn't effective in keeping dangerous infection-causing bacteria from entering the body, so the idea is to scrub away the dead skin and any germs that are festering there. It's torture for patients.

(Think about how it feels when you burn your finger on an iron and run water over it, then multiply that kind of pain by a million. I've heard about people who are in deep comas and still wince when they're being cleaned.) And it's torture for the nurses and burn techs who are inflicting the pain.

I looked into the smiling eyes of a masked face looking down at me. "It's okay," he said, reassuringly, but I wasn't at all reassured. I didn't know what to expect, but I knew it couldn't be good. It was as if he could read my thoughts, that kindly burn tech. He was a big, burly African American guy, with muscles so big they protruded from the short sleeves of his scrubs, and he held me protectively while they cut off my bandages. "I promise we'll take good care of you," he said.

Someone came at me with scissors and began cutting off all of my bandages. When the bandages were gone, I lay there naked and shivering (the skin also helps control body temperature, but the shivering may have been terror-driven), and they went to work on me. If I could have, I would have screamed bloody murder and begged for more medicine to numb the pain. They sprayed me with warm water and washed

270

my burns with antibacterial soap and small gauze pads, but it felt as if they were raking my raw skin with steel wool. I wanted to get out of there, but every time I tried to move I felt a big, muscled arm come over me to hold me down.

"How can this be helping anything?" I wondered. I don't know how long it lasted, but it felt like hours. By the end, I was a bloody mess. They smothered my burns with rust-colored ointment and wrapped me back up. Good job, they said. See you tomorrow. Tomorrow? Tankings take place at least once every day.

I had trouble sleeping all night, dreading the next time in the torture chamber, but each time I woke up Papa was there in the chair next to my bed, holding my hand.

I felt so safe with Papa and confident that nothing bad would happen to me when he was there, which he was all the time. Even if I hadn't been the most faithful Christian, he prayed for me and for the boys enough for both of us. And I loved him for it.

Papa had his work cut out for him those first days after the crash. Besides sleeping in my room every night (which he did for the next six weeks), he became my official bodyguard. More than once, a reporter snuck onto the floor to try to get a peek at the famous evangelist's poor sick kid, and Papa had to shoo them off, but the real problem was well-meaning religious crackpots who came to pray over me. One day, when Papa had flown back to Dallas for a few hours to take care of some ministry business, a nurse peeked into my room and asked if I was expecting company. No, I said. She said that she'd stopped a man and a woman outside my door. The woman was rotund and unkempt, with greasy hair and missing teeth. She told the nurse she was a self-ascribed prophetess with prayer power and she was there to heal me. I shook my head. "I think I'll pass," I said. The nurse went back to the couple and pointed toward the exit. "Out!" she said. "And don't come back."

Papa always kept watch at my door after that.

During that month I spent in the Kansas City hospital, I was always asking for the doctor, and when he came I pitched as many questions as he was willing to answer. Some of my scribbles were clear-headed and almost legible. Others were confused and unreadable. Once, after I had complained about a lightning-hot pain radiating through my core, he changed my pain medication, causing me to write: "This is not the right med, it hurts more." Another time I wrote, "My arm and head shouldn't be burning." And, "Where's Pop?" I guess I meant Papa, as I'd never called him Pop before.

I insisted on making my own medical calls and stubbornly clung to the shred of independence I had left by calling the shots and leaving my parents out of my decisions. My parents were talking about flying in my brother and sister to see me that first week, and I wrote with ferocity, "NO! I don't want them to see me like this!" My fear was that Charity and Cameron would be terrified of the way I looked and run away from my wretched-looking body.

Writing sapped me of what little energy I had, and Mom developed another way to help me communicate. She drew boxes on pieces of paper. One might say "Yes," and the other "No." One might say "Stay?" and another, "Go?" meaning did I want her to spend the night or to leave me alone with my thoughts? I usually didn't have to answer that one because Papa slept in the chair by my bed every night, except for the days he had to fly back to Dallas on business or to Oklahoma to speak at the funerals for each of the boys. I was bitter about not being able to go with him, but I was too sick and still hooked up to the ventilator.

At the beginning of my recovery, my main goal was getting off the ventilator so I could speak. The doctors' concern was my collapsed lung and whether my good lung could support my breathing. I was intent on proving that I was mentally aware and physically stable enough to have the breathing tube removed. After a couple of days, he agreed that we could give it a try.

Having the tube removed felt like a gigantic slug being pulled out of my gut. I gasped, my heart rate skyrocketed, and I started gagging. As soon as it was out, I tried talking, but the nurse who was attending to me told me to stay quiet. My throat was filled with phlegm and who knows what other kinds of crap. They called Mom into the room. I tried talking again, but the only thing that came out was this raspy rumble. "I'm here, Mom," I said. It was frightening, hearing my voice, and I asked for my paper and pen. I wrote a note to the doctor. "Listen to me. I'm growling."

The doctor said I would be able to talk soon enough. My voice box was irritated from the tube. It would take a few days to heal and then I'd have my voice back. But I couldn't wait. There was something I needed to say.

# 26
## Do You Want to Know What Happened?

When we honestly ask ourselves which persons in our lives mean the most to us, we often find that it is those who, instead of giving advice, solutions, or cures, have chosen rather to share our pain and touch our wounds with a warm and tender hand.
— HENRI J. M. NOUWEN, *THE ROAD TO DAYBREAK: A SPIRITUAL JOURNEY*

I woke up in the middle of the night. I knew it was sometime between midnight and daybreak because the sights and sounds of the hospital were different then. The lights were dimmed to an eerie blue, and the hallway was quiet except for the occasional static voice coming over the public address system. The moment I opened my eyes, the crashing plane and frightened faces of the boys flooded my thoughts. I tried to beat back the flashbacks, but they overpowered me, and I felt terribly alone and afraid. Papa wasn't there the way he always was. He'd traveled out of town that night to speak at Austin's funeral the next day. He'd been asked to speak at services for all four of the boys. Of course he had to go. I wish I could have, and I was filled with regret that I would never have a chance to say a proper good-bye.

I listened intently for footsteps in the hall. Nurses and technicians were always coming into and going out of the room at night. Now I heard nothing, no signs of life at all. Tears streamed down the sides of my face. I still couldn't speak except for an occasional word that sounded more like a rusty grunt. I was afraid to be alone with my thoughts, they were dark and forbidding, and I was whimpering like a frightened child. Of all nights for Papa to be gone, I thought. I needed to tell someone my story now and there was no one to tell.

The nurse's bell was out of my reach, and panic stabbed at my gut. I was feeling anxious and desperate. I tried making myself sleep. Counting sheep? It was no use. Every time I closed my eyes fiery ghouls and bloody ghosts visited me. My heart rate spiked. Couldn't anyone hear the racing rate of my heart on the monitor? A moment passed, an endless moment, and one of my favorite nurses walked into the room. She was clocking out for the night and wanted to check on me before she left, she said. "Is everything okay, Hannah?" she asked. She saw my tears and asked if I was in pain. I shook my head. No more than usual.

My heart had settled down a bit. She turned on the track lights in the room and stood over me, looking at me with the kindest eyes. I was alone in the room, because the patient who had been on the other side of the divider curtain, whose burns were less severe than mine, had caught an infection and died the day before. I think the nurse could see the desperation on my face.

I hadn't been able to tell anyone about the crash, how it happened or what I experienced, and I needed to get it out. I had to talk about it, even if I couldn't talk. I felt more coherent than I had since I'd been in the hospital, and I was afraid if I didn't tell someone right then my story would be lost in a morphine haze again, and who knew for how long? The longer I held my story in, the more I succumbed to the debilitating sadness that followed me. I wanted to be with the boys, not recovering in the hospital. I didn't want to live without them. I wanted to be dead with them. Sharing my burden with someone would be honoring them. Because then people would know that my friends died heroes. And they died with God in their hearts.

I motioned to the nurse to hand me my pad of paper and pencil. I did my best to scratch out my request. "I have to tell you what happened to me." She looked at me quizzically, and I handed her my first note. She squinted as she looked at the paper, and I knew she was trying to decipher my words. Did she understand? I wondered. She began sounding out my attempt at words. "Call? . . . No, tell . . . happy . . . happened? . . . You want to tell me what happened?" she asked, finally. I nodded vigorously.

The nurse pulled a chair up to my bed. I knew her shift was ending, but she didn't seem to be in a rush to leave. I began jotting down more notes, sometimes only a couple of words per piece of paper. I knew some of the words were no more legible than scribbles, but I was determined to say what I had to say, whether she understood or not.

I wrote for what seemed like an hour or more, and it may have been even longer. *Someone turned on the heater . . . Smoke flew out of the vents . . . Terrible smell . . . That's what Hell smells like . . . My friend Luke made a valiant attempt at getting the plane on the ground . . . We'd nosedived, then tumbled across a Kansas plain and how those final moments seemed never to end . . . I was stuck inside the burning plane . . . Had it not been for my friend, Garrett, who cracked open the door of the plane just before we hit the ground, neither I nor our friend Austin could have gotten out of the burning wreckage.*

I told the nurse that I was grateful for the fireman who taught me when I was a child to stop, drop, and roll if I was on fire, because if he hadn't taught me that I would have run and fanned the flames and been burned even worse than I was. I told her about how I first saw Austin and how my life had been saved because of his persistence and presence. And I explained how Austin, my beloved friend, had given me hope until those sweet ladies in the minivan found us and got us help. Otherwise, I would surely have given up and died.

The nurse nodded, and I saw tears in her eyes. Then I cried again, too. The sun was rising when I put down my pen, too tired to write anymore. I wasn't sure how much my wonderful nurse understood of what I wrote. But, if nothing else, she seemed to understand that we were crying over some

very special boys. And that was enough for
me.

# 27
## FOUR FUNERALS

Every man dies but not every man truly
lives.

— AUSTIN ANDERSON'S FAVORITE
QUOTATION, FROM THE MOVIE
*BRAVEHEART*

### RON'S STORY

The funerals began five days after the crash.
Four funerals in four days. I was asked to
speak at all of them, and, as much as I
didn't want to leave Hannah's bedside, I
wanted to comfort the families and honor
those wonderful young men.

I did my best to give some peace to the
families. I could only imagine the heartache
they felt. Hannah's life had been spared,
and even though we knew she had a long
and troubled road to travel, at least we still
had her to hug and to care for. We could
still hear her voice and try to cheer her when
she was sad. I could still hold her hand

when she woke up tearful and afraid.

Austin and Garrett and Stephen and Luke were four extraordinary young men. They were on their way to rescue a generation, quintessential soldiers in the battle for souls. What happened didn't make sense, and that's what I said at their funerals. Only the Lord knew why they were gone. It was up to all of us to keep them alive in our memories.

Luke was an avid pilot who was pursuing a career in aviation. His family said he had a joy for life and loved helping people. In his obituary, they wrote, "For those that knew Luke, words like spiritual, godly, intelligent, kind, and humble only start to describe the kind of man he was." I added "courageous." I'm sure he was barely clinging to consciousness, with the smoke pouring in his face, but he held on long enough to get that plane on the ground.

Stephen had a wonderful smile that started with his eyes. He was on the Cheer Team at ORU and had graduated with Luke and Austin a week before the crash. He led a youth group at his hometown church and aspired to spend his life witnessing to people. I was proud to have hired him for Teen Mania, and I know he would have made a real difference in the world.

While I was preparing for Garrett's funeral, I learned that one of his favorite quotations was from Jim Elliot, the evangelical missionary who was killed while ministering to a savage tribe in the jungles of Ecuador. "He is no fool who gives what he cannot keep to gain what he cannot lose," Elliot said. It was one of my favorite quotations as well. One of Garrett's own quotations inspired me as much as Elliot's words. "I don't want to save the world," he said in the weeks before he died. "I want to help children every day of my life." Garrett was selfless with his time. His calling was helping children around the world, and his passion was the El Niño Emanuel orphanage in Peru, where he spent vacations adding rooms and donating books and food to help the children living there. I wasn't surprised that more than a thousand mourners came to his funeral at the chapel at ORU. Speaking to them, I said, "Today we have a fallen soldier. My question to all of us: Who will rise to take his place?"

Who would rise to take all of their places?

The hardest funeral for me was Austin's. Every news organization had picked up on the interviews about him pulling Hannah from the burning plane. He'd been lauded as a hero in virtually every story about the crash. As far as his family knew, the news reports were true.

I'd read a news interview with Austin's fiancée, Elizabeth. It was heartbreaking.

The story said, in part:

Elizabeth rushed to a Kansas hospital to be at Austin's bedside.

"It was hard, because it didn't look like him," she said.

That night — with a broken heart — she knew was the long good-bye.

"It was so hard to say good-bye," she said. "I kept leaving the room, went back in the room. All I could tell him was how proud I was of him, that I loved him so much, and I was so sorry this happened to him."

Elizabeth says Austin lived with purpose. She says the former Marine set out to graduate from ORU because he promised his father he would. Austin graduated from ORU one week prior to his death.

Although Austin was badly burned in the crash, he carried Hannah from the wreckage. She is the only survivor.

Family and friends say he's a hero, but Elizabeth says Austin has always been, and will always be her hero.

"It's moments like that where true character is really revealed," she said. "That's who he was."

It all started with that one quote from Austin's friend. "She couldn't talk, but they gave her a pen and paper and all she wrote, over and over, was "Austin saved me. Austin saved me," she told a reporter.

I'm sure her intentions were pure and good. But the story just wasn't true.

On the night before the funeral, Hannah told the story of the crash for the first time to a nurse and, the next morning, on the day of Austin's funeral, she told it again and in more detail to Katie, while I listened in by speakerphone. As Hannah wrote, and Katie translated her notes, it became clear that Austin hadn't pulled her from the wreckage. She had climbed out herself and was yards away, alone in a cornfield, when she turned and saw Austin stumbling from the plane. The fact that he hadn't rescued Hannah from the plane certainly didn't make him any less a hero to us or to her. He'd kept her calm and led her to the road, and she credited him with saving her life.

But I was headed into a room full of people who'd believed what they'd read in the news accounts and wanted to hear more about it from me. The task before me was

286

difficult and awkward. I wanted to somehow prepare Austin's loved ones, before the funeral, that they wouldn't be hearing a harrowing story of Austin pulling Hannah from the plane.

I met his family in the back room of their church in Enid, Oklahoma, before the funeral. We were all hugging, and I was trying to comfort them as best I could. I could feel their anticipation, so I said, "You know, we're still figuring out what the real story is. We're sure Austin helped in some way."

The funeral was standing room only. The whole town came out for Austin, and the Marines were represented well. Soldiers in full uniform carried Austin's coffin into the church. I felt such pride. I walked to the lectern with trepidation when it was my turn to speak. I asked the Lord to help me with the words. After a brief silence, I said how Austin had talked to me about how Hannah had saved him when he returned from war by helping him to process his feelings and encouraging him about his faith. I said, "So we're not really sure exactly what happened in those final moments, but I'm confident that, in the end, Austin returned the favor." Everyone in the church jumped to their feet and cheered Austin, and that is how it should have been.

Ironically, we later learned that both the medical examiner and the fire chief believe Austin tried to save Stephen. Stephen's body was found outside the plane, on the port side, and his body was less burned than all of the others. In a letter to the Marine Corps, requesting that Austin be recognized for making "the supreme sacrifice," Chief Duane Banzet wrote: "When the coroner's findings of cause of death for the three men was made known to me, it was clear that Staff Sergeant Anderson had to have attempted to remove from harm Stephen Luth, as he was killed instantly (in the crash) and there is no possible way he could have crawled to his position (outside the plane) as he was already dead."

That didn't surprise me. I knew Austin. He was a hero. He would give his life for his country and he would give his life for a friend.

# 28

# NIGHTMARES, FLASHBACKS, AND A FRIGHTENING REALITY

Hell is a state of mind — ye never said a truer word.

— C. S. LEWIS, *THE GREAT DIVORCE*

The flashbacks and nightmares kept coming while I was in the hospital. I'd imagine that Austin and I were in the cornfield. It's just him and me under a dazzling blue summer sky. He's smiling that "I love life" smile of his, the one that reminds me of sunshine. His brown eyes sparkle and his nose crinkles up, and he holds out his hand to me.

"May I have this dance?" he asks. "Of course!" I say. I fall into his sturdy tan arms, completely content to be with my dear friend. That's when I realize we are both naked and covered with blood.

I was terrified of sleep because I knew the next nightmare would be even worse than the one before. They always were. I'd see myself back in the burning plane, draped over Garrett's lifeless body, when he'd jerk his head up and begin talking to me, as if we were back under the Forty-first Street Bridge, smoking cigars and drinking cans of Pabst Blue Ribbon beer. Or I'd dream I was hobbling away from the fiery plane as it was about to explode. I was almost far enough away to survive the blast when the movie in my mind would rewind, and I'd begin running backward toward the crash with no way to stop the film.

After every terrible dream, I woke up on soaked sheets, screaming. What was even more horrifying than those gruesome, frightful images were the times when I woke up from a good dream, a dream about laughing at one of Austin's jokes, or walking hand-in-hand with Garrett through a park beside a river, and then realized that my reality was my nightmare.

One of my many dreams was a recurring one, and I HATED HAVING IT. Every time I did it took days to recover from it. In this dream, I'm frolicking in a meadow, and I notice there's a little medieval festival going on nearby. It's like a scene out of *The Chronicles of Narnia,* with magicians and mythical beasts and talking animals and a big feast spread out over a long, wooden table in the middle of it all. People are playing musical instruments and skipping and dancing through the tall, verdant grass, and the women all have fresh, pastel-colored flowers in their hair. I join them, and they welcome me with applause. I'm running and leaping through the field with the others, my heart bursting with the joy of a blissful child. I feel so beautiful. My skin is like milk, soft and fluid. And my body feels like the body of a dancer, nimble, lithe, free. *This must be Heaven,* I think. *But where is God?*

That's when I wake up to my living nightmare. I can't move my limbs, and my body throbs with the pain of my burns. I am alone in my room, without the comforting presence of my family or my friends. I wonder if I will ever be able to run through a field, or dance, or love. I want to know when — if — I will ever look in the mirror and see myself as I once was. Healthy. Undamaged. Whole.

The dream reminded me of everything I couldn't do that I once could. It reminded me of everything — and I loathed this thought — that I feared I would never do again. So therein lay my dilemma. I slept to escape my reality, but I fought sleep to avoid the nightmares that awakened me to my nightmare. I was trapped in my own personal Hell, one that I did not choose for myself, thank you, C. S. Lewis.

Even the drugs I took for the pain — and they were potent and addictive — didn't give me respite from my grim perception of reality. The drugs made me delusional and gave me psychedelic hallucinations. At first they were vivid, wildly colored dreams, but then the beautiful colors darkened and became tainted and murky. In one hallucination, I was at a freak show. The whole show was colored with bright, matted cloth made from different kinds of material, brocades and silks and lamés and swanskin. The ringmaster, a little person, was navigating me and pointing out all the different characters. A four-legged woman. A human unicorn. A bearded lady. A boy with the face of a horse. I heard circus sounds, elephants trumpeting, lions roaring, the crack of the trainers' whips and the rapid-fire chant of an auctioneer. Beautiful white pearls and colorful jewels of all shapes and sizes were everywhere, and the ringmaster encouraged me to stuff my pockets with them, which I did, but then I put all of them back, because they weren't mine to take. The further into the show we got, the narrower and dirtier it got, and I began to see its real colors, which were dark and murky. The ringmaster got shorter and shorter, shrinking with every step, and his voice, which had been friendly and welcoming, dropped menacingly. I didn't understand what had changed. Then the ringmaster leaned in close to my face and told me why I was there. He wanted me to be part of the show. Because I was a freak.

There were times that the hallucinations blended with reality. When I was first hospitalized, someone had tied a Get Well Happy Face balloon to a post near the foot of my bed. It was an eerie, burnt yellow, shiny Happy Face with little circus flags around it, making it look like a Happy Face sunshine. I was barely lucid at the time, but I hated that balloon, and it became a character in a lot of my dreams.

I'm still fuzzy about a lot of my early days in the hospital, but I remember I had this one nurse. She was really young, with dark hair and long, polished nails. I thought she was gorgeous, but she was really mean to me. She treated me as if I was mentally retarded, and sometimes she became impatient with me, as if it was my fault that my body smelled like burned flesh and waste and I couldn't do anything for myself. I couldn't even talk, because I had a breathing tube jammed in my throat, and when I motioned for something — usually I was just looking for a reassuring smile — she'd yell at me, saying, "What? I don't understand what you want!" Of course, I couldn't tell anyone, because I couldn't talk, but I dreaded every time she was on the floor.

I can't swear to every detail of those early memories, so I'm keeping a lot of them to myself, but the next part of my story — as confirmed by my mom — is completely accurate. After one of my skin graft surgeries, unbeknownst to me, I was moved to a different room. When I awakened, everything looked different — the placement of the window, the pictures on the wall, the furniture, everything except the scary Happy Face balloon tied near the foot of my bed. And the mean nurse. I thought I was having a nightmare, and I kept opening and closing my eyes, trying to change the dream. When it didn't happen, I got really frustrated. My mom was in the room, and I tried wiggling whatever I could to get her attention. I'm gesturing to say, "Get the restraints off! I feel like I'm in prison. I'm trapped!"

Mom hadn't expected that I'd wake up so quickly. I saw the terror in her eyes the same moment she saw the terror in mine. She ordered the nurse to loosen the restraints.

"Please," she said. "Take them off now. She's awake and she's afraid."

That nurse was so patronizing. She talked to me as if I were two, not twenty-two. Looking down at me with her big hair and her cat eyes, she asked, "Now, Hannah. Are you going to be a good girl? If I free your hands, you're not going to pull your breathing tube out, are you?"

I shook my head no. How I hated that woman. Why in the world was she a nurse? I wondered. She obviously hated her job.

With my hands free, I pointed to the balloon. "So you like the balloon," she asked, her big, fake smile more for my mom's benefit than mine. I pointed to the balloon again, poking my finger harder in the air. Mom looked puzzled. She handed me a piece of paper and a pencil. "What is it, honey?" she asked.

I drew a circle and pointed at the balloon. *Get it out!*

The balloon was taken away, and the nurse turned to look at the monitor beeping above my head, because my heart was racing. When she did, I drew an arrow on the paper that pointed to the nurse and hoped my eyes said what my mouth couldn't.

*Get her out, too! I don't like her! She's mean.*

# 29
# HEALING

"Hearts are breakable," Isabelle said. "And I think even when you heal, you're never what you were before."

— CASSANDRA CLARE,
*CITY OF FALLEN ANGELS*

Toward the end of May, the doctors were talking about releasing me from the burn unit in Kansas City and sending me to a rehabilitation hospital in Dallas. I had been through thirty hours of skin graft surgeries on my back, right arm, and leg, and I looked like a bad patch job. At one point I had temporary skin on my arm from an African American cadaver. My skin is as white as snow, so it hardly matched, but I liked it. I called myself Calico Hannah.

I was thankful to be alive (sometimes) and I tried being upbeat for the sake of my family, but the pain from my burns and my surgeries, coupled with my emotional agony, made me pretty unpleasant to deal with sometimes. The doctors and nurses in the burn unit had more patience than anyone I'd ever met before. It's amazing what they deal with every day, the terrible things they see, yet they still continue to smile. I couldn't have imagined just how debilitating being burned could be until it happened to me. I was maimed, and the physical and psychological toll it took was mind-boggling.

In his dispatches to the ministry, Papa always put a good face on my progress, but his positive thoughts weren't necessarily my thoughts, and I often critiqued them when I was alone in my room.

"Thank you all for praying for Hannah — I can't tell you all how much it means," he wrote on his blog in the third week of May. "Hannah went through a five-and-a-half-hour surgery yesterday. The doctors said she did very well, and they did a lot of skin grafting. The whole process causes extreme pain for her, so since the surgery, she has been pretty heavily sedated (*translation: completely out of it!*). She is on a ventilator again for the next couple of days, and tomorrow she goes in for another skin graft surgery. (*Woohoo!*) We think that may be the last one she'll need to have. (*Praise Lord God!*)

"I stayed the night in the room with her after her surgery, just to be with her (*Papa is an angel*) and she slept very well. (*Not! I never sleep well, even when I'm as drugged up as Lindsay Lohan on her worst day!*) A few times she woke up, and of course with a breathing apparatus, she can't talk. (*Lucky you, Papa! I had a lot to say! 'More meds, please!'*) So, she's trying to write notes, expressing what she needs or how we can help her. (*Get me outta here!!!*)"

A few days after that, Papa updated his blog with this note:

"I want to thank you all so much for praying! As we have heard from people praying from all around the world for Hannah's recovery, she continues to be in the burn center of the KU Medical Center in Kansas City and is making significant progress. She's still in quite a bit of pain, but she is beginning to use her limbs more." (*If that meant wiggling my fingers and my toes!*)

The doctors got me up and out of bed after my last surgery in June, and they had me taking a couple of steps at a time around my bed. Those small steps took everything out of me. I was so weak and so exhausted that afterward I collapsed on my bed. After that, I had to take a few extra steps every day. Every step felt like a mile. I wasn't always the most willing patient, but I tried.

On the first Saturday in June, three weeks after the crash, I walked all the way to the visitors' area and back, for the first time without a walker. The doctors saw that as significant progress.

Two days later, I was being loaded into a medical transport plane, headed to a rehabilitation hospital in Dallas. They gave me extra sedation because I was petrified of the plane, but the medication did little to blunt my frazzled nerves. Wouldn't you know it? The weather was bad, and the plane was dodging thunderstorms all the way to Dallas. Papa and a medical technician took turns holding my hand the whole way. Afterward, Papa wrote on his blog that we had an "an amazing adventure." Leave it to Papa to look on the bright side. I called it a punishment worse than Hell.

We landed in Dallas, and I was whisked to Zale Lipshy University Hospital.

Things were going pretty well until my doctor came into the room. When I saw him I gasped. He looked just like Garrett, and he even had his mannerisms. I began to cry.

"I'm sorry," he said. "What's the matter?" I tried to explain, but every time I did I burst into tears again. "I can't," I said. "You can't be my doctor." I'll bet he'd never heard that before. Papa's timing is always impeccable, and he walked in right as I was sobbing. I saw the doctor look at him with an expression of complete bewilderment. Papa knew right away what I was thinking. The doctor really did look that much like Garrett. "It's not personal," Papa said. "I'm sorry. She's been through a lot today." (I ended up sticking with the doctor, and I'm glad I did. He was awesome.)

Papa dried my eyes and pointed out the stack of cards and letters from well-wishers that awaited me — as in Kansas City, many from people I didn't know.

I couldn't believe it when he showed me the newspaper stories about my progress and the move to Dallas. I had no idea so many people were following my recovery. Papa said he had even been interviewed by Matt Lauer for the *Today Show* that morning, and I thought that was pretty cool.

As grateful as I was to be one step closer to home, I was still in terrible pain. My limbs ached from the wounds and the lack of movement, and the physical therapists put me to work right away. They were like drill sergeants, but with hearts. When I didn't feel like working, they pushed me harder. *Reach those arms! Throw that ball! Climb those stairs! Stretch!* The danger of not doing the exercises was that my skin would tighten and my scars would thicken and constrict, and I'd be in danger of permanently losing the movement in my hand, arm, and leg.

One day, the doctor took my cane away. I knew I didn't need it anymore, but it had become a crutch. (I was developing a lot of crutches.) I argued at first, but he wouldn't budge. If I was angry, he said, I should write my feelings on the mirror in the therapy room. "And reach high when you do," he said. "Stttttrrrrretch that arm!"

I took a marker and wrote until my arm throbbed.

"I hate this place."

"I hate the doctors and the therapists."

"I hate my skin."

"I hate myself."

"I miss my friends! They're gone! Is it my fault? Why couldn't I save them? Why wasn't I stronger?"

"Why didn't I let Garrett into my heart?"

"Why wasn't I honest about my true emotions?"

"What am I supposed to do?"

I felt better for a while.

For three weeks I did what they told me. I hated every minute of it, but I knew I had to do what they said. In early July, after a month of physical and occupational therapy, the doctors said I was ready to go home. I had made good progress, they said, and I could continue my physical therapy as an outpatient while I was living at home with my parents. Even though I hated the hospital, I begged them to let me stay. I needed more help, I said. I needed to be in a hospital setting. I wouldn't do as well at home. "Please," I cried. "Just a little bit longer. Please let me stay."

The truth was, I was terrified of going home. At least when I was in the hospital, and then in the rehabilitation center, I always had something to distract me from thinking about things. There was always another surgery, or another vial of blood being drawn, or exercise to perform, or a stranger trying to get into my room.

At home, I wouldn't have those diversions. There would be no escape from my tortured thoughts. Except for the pills that helped me to forget. And I'd made sure I stockpiled plenty of them.

# 30
## TURNING POINT

The darker the night, the brighter the stars.
The deeper the grief, the closer is God!
— FYODOR DOSTOYEVSKY,
*CRIME AND PUNISHMENT*

After nearly a month at the hospital in Dallas the doctors said there was no reason to keep me anymore. I could do physical and occupational therapy three times a week as an outpatient. Papa came to take me home in his pickup truck. I was mad at the doctor for making me go and I stalled all morning, trying to hold off the inevitable trip back to Garden valley. When I was finally wheeled out of the hospital, I felt like a sickly baby bird that'd been pushed out of the nest. I brought a bunch of pillows from the hospital with me. Papa piled them on the passenger-side seat, and two aides helped me up into the truck. Poor Papa. He was so excited that I was coming home, but

I was in a grouchy mood and didn't want to engage him in any kind of conversation.

We got on the road and, as I stared out the passenger-side window, Papa put on some eighties music and sang along with the radio. He was upbeat and acting corny and I knew he was trying to make me smile, just as he had always done when I was a little girl and we were alone together in the car. He was trying his best to cheer me up, but there was no lifting my spirits. I was terrified of going back home to a quiet room, where everything was peaceful and calm, and there was nothing to distract me from finally facing my reality, a reality in which I would have to deal with the absence of my beloved friends, my guilt over their deaths, and living in my new pockmarked skin.

We stopped at a coffee house on the way, another gesture by Papa to try to make me happy. He knew about my obsession with coffee and how I loved spending time in coffee houses. I was hardly healed enough to enjoy anything, though. I had tubes in my nose and my burns still bled through my bandages. I was heavily medicated and in terrible pain and I couldn't walk more than a few steps without having to rest. Papa gently pulled me out of the cab of the truck and loaded me into a wheelchair he'd rented for such times. (A wheelchair? So this is my future, I thought. I can hardly wait to get started.)

Papa steered the chair toward the coffee house. It seemed as if he hit every bump in the pavement, which caused me excruciating pain. A few feet from the door, he came close to running me off the sidewalk, and my face reddened with anger. "Papa!" I cried. "You'd be a terrible nurse!" Papa. Dear Papa. He had the patience of a saint. "That's why I'm a preacher!" he said cheerfully. I made a weak attempt at a smile.

I knew Papa meant well. He always meant well. But I was in no frame of mind to want to hear his jokes, much less to laugh at them. I was so bitter that my mouth tasted sour. I just wanted to take my medication and lapse into nothingness. I gritted my teeth and sipped my coffee as slowly as I could to delay the trip home as long as I possibly could. Finally, I couldn't pretend anymore. I was slurping the last vestiges of my drink long after the drink was gone. Papa stood to leave. "Time to get home," he said. "Mmmhmm," I said.

He pushed me back outside and we hit the same bumps that we did on the way in. When he lifted me back up into the truck, I burst into tears. Papa thought he'd hurt me, and he had, unintentionally, of course. I was crying because everything hurt me. I couldn't even touch my burned fingers to a keyboard on a computer without crying out in pain, and nearly a third of my body was in the same challenged condition. Every pain and every stain reminded me of my fear that I would never live another day without worrying about blood seeping through my clothes, or the slightest touch by someone or something sending me into a tailspin. Papa took my hand in his. I could see his eyes welling with tears. "Give it to the Lord, sweetheart," he said. I cried even harder.

I looked at my father differently after the crash. He had such a purposeful life, a life overflowing with love in and love out. I reveled at his unshakable belief in the word of God and the peace that seemed to come with a life anchored in faith, and I respected him for living within the tenets of his faith. I realized that I had been so angry with him for so long that I'd stopped looking at the sum of who he was, and was only seeing the things I didn't like about what he believed.

Papa was a kind and compassionate man with a huge heart and a silly, goofy streak. He truly cared about people, and he went out of his way to be the best father and husband he could possibly be. How could I be so angry with this loving man who had slept in a chair by my bed for weeks on end, holding my hand and comforting me, even when it meant endless sleepless nights for him? How could I resent him for wanting the religious faith for me that had brought him such comfort and joy during his life?

At the same time I realized I felt disconnected from God because of Papa. He and my mother saw everything in life through the paradigm of their very specific religious beliefs. There wasn't room in their lives for people or ideals that didn't conform to their exacting definition of God. I didn't relate to that God, the one who judged so harshly, and discriminated against perfectly good and decent people, and invited only a privileged few into the kingdom of Heaven. But maybe that didn't mean I couldn't believe.

I had quietly begun wondering if maybe I could rediscover my faith. Perhaps it would just look different from theirs. I couldn't condone the judgments that came with their religious conviction, or the God who rejected good people because they loved someone of their own sex and condemned us for endorsing creative expression in certain music and movies and art. I suspected any God I put my faith in would accept all of us, with all of our human foibles and missteps. And I had started to wonder if He had been with me all the time and I just hadn't allowed myself to see the beauty and breadth of His reach because of the narrow lens I had been given through which to see Him.

I couldn't tell Papa any of that. He wouldn't have been happy that I'd begun thinking about faith again, not unless it was on his terms. No, if I'd told Papa about how my faith was changing and evolving, he'd have been concerned that whatever my beliefs were, they weren't good enough for God. Or for him.

Papa turned his truck into our driveway. "Here we are!" he said. I had gotten completely lost in my thoughts and didn't realize we were so close to home. "Here we are," I said echoing him, trying to muster some enthusiasm.

Mom was waiting at the door. She embraced me, careful not to hurt my burned arm and back. The dogs raced around in circles when they saw me. Charity was living in Chicago, but I'd been hoping my brother would be there to greet me, but no such luck. Papa said Cameron was away at summer camp. The house was, as I'd expected, as peaceful and quiet as a Zen garden. I panicked and went straight to my room.

Mom had tidied it up and it smelled like sweet lavender. The windows were propped open and a slight breeze blew the lacy curtains inward. Mom had moved my favorite armchair in from the living room, a beautiful antique that had once belonged to my great-grandmother, and she'd placed chocolates on my pillow, just like in a fancy hotel. My private bath had a shower chair and seven different kinds of creams lined up on the vanity. (Mom and Papa, unbeknownst to each other, had both shopped for creams for me for my homecoming, knowing that part of my therapy was keeping my healing skin moisturized.)

While Papa propped up the pillows on my bed, Mom walked in with a tray with home-made soup and an English muffin with peanut butter, my favorite snack. She set it down on my night table and hugged me. "I need to take a nap," I said. Mom nodded. "Of course, sweetheart," she said.

Closing the bedroom door behind my parents, I took the bowl of soup and dumped it in the toilet, then wrapped the English muffin in a napkin, crumpled it into a ball and hid it under my bed. I hadn't had an appetite since the crash and now my stomach was in knots because I was home, and I feared I might be sick if I even attempted to force something down.

Later that night, after my parents turned in for the night, I snuck into the kitchen and tossed my balled-up muffin into the trash. The house was pitch dark and the only sound was the ticking of the grandfather clock. The silence made me cry. "The world is closing in on me," I thought. "I feel like I'm suffocating." I walked back to my room and tried watching *The Scarlet Pimpernel* for the fourth time, but my vision was distorted by flashbacks of burning flesh and bloody limbs. Feelings of panic and desperation enveloped me. I thought I sensed Austin and Garrett in the room, but I wasn't ready to see them, and I told them so. "I'm pretending you're not here," I said. "I know you want a response from me, but I'm not going to talk to you." Were they waiting for an apology? "No," I said. "I'm sorry but I'm not ready to talk to you, not yet, not here."

I turned my attention to the numbers on my alarm clock. How long until it was time for my next round of meds? It was three in the morning and I'd taken my last dose at one. I was taking between sixty and seventy prescribed pills a day for everything from my physical pain to anxiety and depression, and the ones I called my numbing pills always wore off after an hour or so. According to the alarm clock, I still had two hours to go before my next dose. But my skin was crawling.

Minutes passed and I turned up the volume on my TV, trying to drown out my wretched thoughts. My room seemed to be getting smaller and smaller and I felt nauseated. If I didn't get some air, and soon, I knew I'd faint, and then what? Papa wouldn't find me until he came in to say good-bye before he went to work.

Feelings of fear and helplessness overtook me. I was reminded at that moment of how I had lost all control of my life. As if I had ever forgotten. I didn't have power over my body or my thoughts anymore. I had to get out of the house. I left my room and walked outside on the deck and down the steps to the edge of the lake. Leaning against the fence post, I searched the blackened sky for answers. I cried out for Austin and Garrett, and my words echoed across the surface of the lake. "I'm sorry I asked you to go away," I said, sobbing into my hands. "Where are you now? What am I supposed to do without you?" The only sound I heard was silence, and in my grief, I turned to God for comfort. "Please!" I whimpered. "Show me some sign that you're here, that I'm not alone."

I waited for a shooting star, or a clap of thunder. Even a fish jumping out of the water would do. I waited and waited for something, please something, but nothing happened. My mind began churning up dark thoughts, and I blinked to try to force the horrific images away. Even if I'd been successful, I knew it would only be a matter of seconds before those shattering memories flashed in front of my eyes again.

My mind rushed to the pills in my room. My pills, I thought. It was the only control I had left, when I took my meds. I turned and hobbled back up the steps and stumbled into the house. Once I was inside my room, I locked the door behind me, grabbed my bottle of numbing pills, and turned it upside down on my bedspread. I counted out two, then three, and one more for good measure. Soon, I would be drifting off into oblivion.

# 31
## THE SHOWER

Mothers can forgive anything! Tell me all,
and be sure that I will never let you go,
though the whole world should turn from
you.
— LOUISA MAY ALCOTT, *JO'S BOYS*

Looking at my own body triggered some of
my worst flashbacks. I used to have white,
creamy skin. Now a third of it was flaming
red and mottled and scarred. When I looked
in the mirror I felt as if I was seeing someone
else. Every time I looked at myself it was
May 11 again. *Flashback! "Hannah! I want
you to tell me the truth. Do I look okay?" "Yes,
yes, Austin. You look fine."* Sometimes I
tested myself to prove that I really was seeing me. "Okay, I'm going to move my hand
now," I'd tell myself. I'd look down and see
my hand moving, but it didn't resemble the
pretty little porcelain hand I'd had before
the crash, and I refused to accept that it

was really mine now. *Flashback! The palms of my hands sizzle on a hot metal rod I grab to try to hoist myself out of the plane. I am half in and half out, draped over Garrett's back, but something is stopping me from propelling myself any farther forward.*

My first shower after I got home was torture. Mom helped me to prepare for it but I insisted on going in myself.

There's a towel on the floor so I won't slip and a pillow on the chair in the shower because my butt is so burned I can't sit anywhere without a cushion. I don't know what to do first. I turn on the water and hold tight to the chair as the warm water pours over my body. The shower spray feels like prickly needles piercing my skin. I embrace the pain because, just for a moment, it distracts me from my sorrow. And because I feel as if I deserve to be in pain.

I'm terrified to look down, but I do, and I loathe my body. I reach down to my knees and try to scrub away my scars. It's no use, of course. You can't scrub away scars, I know. But how do I live with them? How will anyone ever look at me without grimacing if I can't look at me without grimacing?

I am overcome with rage, rage about what's happened to me, rage over the senselessness of my friends' deaths — and I can't help thinking, "Why did I live and they died?" I slip off the shower chair and crumple in a heap on the tile floor. There's nowhere to go to hide from myself. I close my eyes as tightly as I can but in an instant I see those mournful images. Austin burning alive in the plane. The human torch I saw had to have been him. Garrett slumped over, dead.

I hate my skin because it reminds me. Reminds me of their dreams unrealized, of what they will never become. Because of me? I fear it is. I search my mind again and again for things I could have done differently. It was their idea to travel to Council Bluffs, but what if I had never mentioned my concerns about Teen Mania? What if they'd never met me? What if I'd suggested we drive instead of fly? Would they still be alive today? So many what ifs with no answers.

My body feels as if it's melting inside out from my wrath. I am frozen there, on the shower floor, and I begin to shiver, even though my skin is as blazing hot as if I were being stuck with a branding iron. Pulling my knees toward my chest, I lie there, in a fetal position, weeping wildly. I try to stifle my sobs with my hands, because I don't want my parents to hear.

I hear a knock on the door. "Hannah?" It's Mom. "Hannah, are you all right?" I almost start laughing. Am I all right? *Am I all right?* Of course I'm all right, Mom. I've lost my friends whom I loved with all my heart. My body is so ugly it makes me sick to look at it. I think I'll never stop bleeding and I'm back living in my bedroom, not eating, not sleeping, living from flashback to flashback, and losing myself in pills and whatever else I can get my hands on to help me forget what I can't stop remembering.

Mom opens the shower door.

"Please, Mom, go away," I say. "Get out! This is my time!"

"Please, Hannah," she says. "What's wrong?"

She starts to cry. I don't like disappointing my mom. I don't want to see her hurt, but I can't seem to keep from lashing out.

"Unless I fall, I don't want you in here!" I cry. "I'll let you know when I need you!"

"Hannah. Hannah, honey."

"Get out! I don't want you in here, Mom. I want to be left alone!"

The shower water beat down on me and, after a while, I was all out of tears. I was tired of being in pain, and I felt as if I wasn't healing. Would I ever heal? Would I ever enjoy my life again? Would I ever be able to look at my own body without feeling disgusted? Once I had big dreams. I wanted to finish graduate school, travel the world, look for purpose in my life. I couldn't imagine those dreams were possible now. I wasn't strong enough to overcome my pain, but especially my loss. I would never get over losing my friends. I would always mourn Garrett and Austin. They were gone and my heart had a gaping hole in it. Sometimes when I tried to picture them in my mind, their faces were fuzzy. I couldn't bear the thought of those images fading away.

I called out to my mother. It turned out that she'd been standing outside the door the whole time. She came in and wrapped a towel around me, then helped me to dress my wounds.

# 32
## OUTPATIENT

Sometime I try to cry and laugh like other people, just to see if it feels like anything.
— BLAINE HARDEN,
*ESCAPE FROM CAMP 14: ONE MAN'S REMARKABLE ODYSSEY FROM NORTH KOREA TO FREEDOM IN THE WEST*

I couldn't move any part of my body without pain, so I usually sat in my room, refusing to exert myself beyond walking to the bathroom, or taking an occasional stroll around the yard on Papa's arm. My days consisted of watching my favorite reruns on TV, turning the pages of books I couldn't concentrate on enough to read, and finding creative places to hide my food so Mom wouldn't know I wasn't eating. Sometimes I used Mom's computer to look up things that were relevant to my recovery — for instance, post-traumatic stress syndrome, a psychological condition triggered by a terrifying event that can completely shake up one's life. I had all of the symptoms, the flashbacks, the nightmares, the paralyzing anxiety. My parents suggested I see friends to help me get my mind off the throbbing of my wounds and the pain in my heart, but I usually refused, and even on those rare occasions when people did come to visit, I was usually so out of it I forgot they'd been there.

The only thing that could get me moving was the three times a week when I knew I had physical therapy in Dallas, and then it wasn't the therapy that motivated me. Home was almost an hour's drive from Dallas, so we hired livery drivers to take me to and from my therapy sessions. Those trips were my big adventures, and I really looked forward to them. I could hardly wait for the car to come so I could escape into an alternate universe, where I didn't have to worry about bleeding on my sheets again or staining the towels Mom used to cover the furniture so I didn't stain the wood or upholstery.

The drivers didn't care what I did. They were an assorted bunch, some women, some men, all of them employed by workmen's comp and using their own cars, many that looked as if they might not make it out of the driveway, much less all the way to Dallas. The drivers didn't seem to care if I was in pain or depressed or even if I stained their backseat. They'd drive along, living their lives, and I'd just be along for the ride, enjoying their chitchat, or their quirks, or their private cell phone conversations.

Some of them were real characters. One of my regulars was a woman who I thought was a man for the longest time. She was forty or fifty, with calloused hands and chewed nails and hair that was cut into a mullet. She wore biker clothes and always the same braided leather bolo tie with a silver and gold Texas Star. Her car smelled like cigarettes and alcohol. She took the corners on those country roads like a race-car driver. I'd shut my eyes really tight and hope for the best, but it was better than being at home thinking about what was and what might have been, or feeling as if I was drowning in survivor's guilt.

After a while I began requesting a driver named Teresa. I adored her. She was a large African American woman with an expressive face and a gleaming white smile, and she always told me stories about her kids and her grandkids. She hadn't had an easy life, but she was always warm and cheerful and I came to really like her. To reward me after every physical therapy session, she'd drive to a McDonald's in a ghetto part of northeast Dallas and get a stash of oatmeal raisin cookies. She'd park the car, pull out two cigarettes, one for her, one for me, and we'd sit there smoking and gorging ourselves.

"Now don't you tell your mama what we're doing," she'd say conspiratorially.

"Not a chance," I'd say, flipping my cigarette butt out the window and stuffing the last cookie in my mouth.

Then we'd be back on the road again, headed back to reality.

# 33
## NOT MY FATHER'S GOD

Un-winged and naked, sorrow surrenders
its crown to a throne called grace.
— ABERJHANI,
*THE RIVER OF WINGED DREAMS*

"I have to go back," I told Papa. "If there's
any chance of me getting better, I have to
go to Kansas to the crash site and you have
to let me go." Six months had passed since
I lost my friends. My skin was on the mend
but my heart was still in pieces and I was
overmedicating to cope with my grief and
my guilt. My parents tried to understand,
but I could tell they were becoming frustrated. Mom began saying she was caring
for "drunk Hannah." I couldn't blame her.
Half the time, I couldn't understand my
own slurred words.

Papa and my mother wanted to come with
me to Kansas, but I refused to let them join
me. This is something I need to do by

myself, I said. Somewhere from deep within me I knew that, until I went back to the last place I was with my friends, I couldn't begin to make peace with myself and I'd never be able to move forward. I'd always be the way I was now, an aimless and troubled soul, angry and guilt-ridden, and looking for a purpose, a reason to live.

The way I looked at it was I had four good reasons to want to die. Not a day ended when I hadn't asked myself why I lived when those boys, who were truer and more unswerving in their faith, didn't survive. I was torn apart about not being able to attend their funerals. That I'd never had a chance to say a proper good-bye, and I owed them that, at least. But, even more, I needed to pull myself together to be able to share their stories of heroism and courage and to take up their pursuit of working for a better world. They'd always wanted for me to find my way back to God, and I had to see if it was possible. In the four months I'd been home from the hospital, I'd begun to think about my faith more, and I'd slowly come to the realization that even though I'd been mad at God, even forsaken God, I didn't want a life without having faith. That didn't mean I didn't have doubts, or that I wasn't still struggling with my beliefs, because I was. But I wanted to try.

I left for Kansas the week before Thanksgiving. Along the way, I stopped at a flower shop for a candle to bring with me to the cornfield. I was headed to the crash site to say good-bye to my friends, and that felt sacred to me, but I was also terrified because I didn't know where I stood with them. I needed to find out.

My first stop was in Neodesha, a small town about ten miles south of the crash site. I'd made arrangements to meet with Fire Chief Duane Banzet at the firehouse there. Duane was one of the first responders at the crash, and he'd taken good care of me in the ambulance. He'd even taken the time to drive to Kansas City to see me in the hospital. He was kind and easy to talk to, and I had a million questions for him about things I either couldn't remember or wanted to clarify from that day.

I got there around lunchtime. Duane greeted me with a smile and a bear hug. "You're a sight for sore eyes, Hannah," he said, inviting me into his office. We talked a long time, hours, in fact, until late in the afternoon. How did he first hear about the crash? I asked. How long had it taken him to get there from the firehouse? What was the first thing he saw when he got there? Did he remember how I looked? What did remember about Austin? Did he know Austin was going to die? Did he think I'd make it? Did he recall how long it took for the medical transport helicopter to come? Had he talked with the two women who found us? Duane answered every question with patience and compassion. He even drew a diagram of the plane on the ground and where each of the bodies of my friends had been found. He was matter of fact yet empathetic, and I could tell that he'd been deeply moved by what he witnessed that day.

As we were talking, I looked around his paneled office. It was cozy and inviting and quiet except for the occasional staticky call that came over the scanner. Happy family pictures were scattered on the desk and credenza. I assumed the pictures were of his wife and his children. One was of a girl who looked to be about my age. "My daughter," he said, reading my thoughts. I got the impression from the photographs that Duane had a satisfying life, but I couldn't help noticing that his eyes looked sad. I imagined he'd seen some pretty awful things in his years of service, and he said that he had, more than his share.

Duane said he'd made it his practice never to get personally involved with the people he met on the job, but something was different with me. It had to do with something he saw in my eyes and Austin's eyes on the day of the crash, he said. Even though he knew we were afraid and in pain, our eyes told a story of a certain kind of serenity. Duane called it "the peace of God." I'd seen that same look in Austin's eyes, but I hadn't been able to identify it. My poor friend's body had been ravaged by fire, he was in terrible pain, and I'm sure he knew he was about to die, but the look in his eyes was one of serenity and conviction. Had I witnessed the peace of God in him?

Duane told me a story from when he was fifteen years old. He was working for his grandfather and his uncle on their farm that summer, he said. They'd just finished lunch, and his uncle told him he had had a truckload of grain that needed to be unloaded for feed for the hogs.

"When my uncle went to check on the cows, I climbed up on the truck bed. I never heard my uncle come back, but the next thing I knew, the truck bed was tilting and I was sliding into the bin with the grain. I was buried alive. My mouth was packed with grain and I couldn't breathe. I knew I was going to die, but a sense of peace came over me and I wasn't afraid. Next thing I know, my body's floating upward, through the stars. I was headed to Heaven."

But his uncle brought him back. He said he heard his uncle screaming for him. He'd dug him out of the grain pile alive. He said, years later, when he became a firefighter and tragedy became a regular part of his life, he often thought about the grain accident and asked himself why he'd been spared, yet he couldn't save a child who'd drowned or a baby who'd died from SIDS. Often, he said, he'd asked God, "Why me, and not this little two-year-old or seven-year-old or ten-year-old?" After every loss, he said, he'd be depressed for long periods of time.

"I know you're asking yourself the same thing, Hannah," he said. "Why, God, did You save my life? Why did You give me another chance? Why me and not Austin or Luke or Stephen or Garrett? I know you feel unworthy of being the only one who survived. But what happened isn't your fault."

"Why do you keep doing this job that causes you so much torment?" I asked.

Duane hesitated for a minute. "It's what God wants me to do," he said. "It's not easy for us to understand why this stuff happens, but bad things happen to good people every day. God's got a plan for you and you'll have to ask Him what it is." As if he knew of my struggle to hear God's voice, he added: "Don't expect the heavens to open up and hear Him start talking to you. It doesn't happen that way. It's a kind of peace that comes over you when you're on the right path."

"Did you ever question God?" I asked.

"Still do," he said. "After every kid I lose I ask 'Why?' Never got a good answer yet. But what I do know is that the Lord wants me here to help the next person, to give someone else the second chance He gave me, not to question why He took the last one."

"I want to keep living," I said. "But I don't know how."

Duane smiled a rueful smile. "Hannah," he said. "Your life has changed, no doubt about it, but it doesn't have to be bad. You need to grieve the boys, to talk to them, to say 'good-bye.' But at some point, you've got to let them go and find the courage to get on with your life. That's how you keep their memory alive."

"Will you come with me to the crash site, Duane?" I asked.

■ ■ ■ ■

We arrive just as the sun is dipping below the horizon. Duane understands that, although I am glad for his company, I need to take this last part of my journey alone. He points me in the direction I want to go and as he waits on the side of the gravel road, I head off through the cornfield. The only sound I hear is that of the dried cornstalks snapping under my feet. It's too quiet and I fight off flashbacks of the plane roaring across the field and into the red oak, and all the carnage that followed.

I'm fighting the urge to turn back when I'm suddenly aware of what feels like a hand on my back. I turn, briefly, expecting to see Duane. He must have been worried about letting me walk through the field alone. But no one's there. No one I can see. Something, it feels like a slight wind at my back, gently pushes me forward. I am not moving against my will, but, at the same time, I feel as if I'm not making the choice to go forward. I am going where I'm going. Period. I'm not frightened anymore and, strangely, my sadness has abated and I'm eager to see what's coming. I've lost all concept of time and place. Then, in the blackness of night, on the ground in front of me I see the tiny, shimmering pieces of the metal left over from the plane. In a strange way, I feel as if I'm home. I lay my blanket out in front of the towering oak tree, its trunk still charred from the fire.

In the near distance, I heard the howl of a pack of coyotes and I begin to sing with them, but my song is one my sister Charity wrote for me after the crash.

And we'll walk on holy ground,
Clothed in celestial sound
And when sorrow falls
I'm going to cry tears of joy.

I light my candle and instantly feel the presence of Garrett and Austin. Their spiritual presence is heavy, like a blanket covering me, and I can't deny it. It's almost as if they're weighing me down and passing through me to prove to me, doubting Hannah, that they're here. They're really here. I feel joy. Complete and utter joy. "I hoped you'd be here. I knew you would be. You've always been there when I needed you and I've never needed you more than I do now."

I talk to them for a long while, telling them everything that, before now, I could only write in my journal. About how much

I love them and how I wonder what they would think of my life now, and how I can't promise I can go on without them, not the way they'd like for me to go on. I ask for their forgiveness and I know their response. I don't need to see their faces or hear their voices. I just know. I just believe.

*We're happy, Hannah. Really happy. We're where we want to be. We know we encouraged you, supported you, enriched your life. But some things you need to discover on your own. You need to be able to figure things out for yourself. You can mourn, and we love that you do, but you can't mourn forever. You have to dance.*

I think about the lyrics of my sister's song.

. . . I'm going to dance
Oh, I will dance.

I promise them I'll try.

After a while, I fold my blanket, collect my candle, and begin the long walk back to the gravel road where Duane is waiting. The pieces of the plane that I'd collected jingle in my pocket and I smile. The boys are okay and I will be okay, too. I know that now.

For the first time in my life I accept that sometimes I have to believe what I cannot hear and what I cannot see. The light of the moon shines on my face and I'm overtaken by a sense of tranquility, a kind of tranquility I have never felt before. And then I realize that what I'm feeling is the warmth and the tranquility of faith.

# 34
# I'M BACK

And a step backward, after making a wrong turn, is a step in the right direction.
— KURT VONNEGUT, *PLAYER PIANO*

Cameron had something on his mind. I knew my little brother better than anyone, and his face betrayed his silence. As soon as he walked into my room less than a week after my visit to the crash site, I could see he was troubled by something, really troubled. "What's wrong, Cammy?" I asked. He hemmed and hawed and shuffled his feet a bit. I knew he wanted to say something, but he was having trouble getting the words out, so I persisted. "Really, what's the matter?" Reluctantly, he pulled out his phone and pushed a button. "Hey that's me!" I said, hearing my own voice. My smile faded to dismay and then embarrassment as I heard one word slur into the next. I sounded drunk and I was blabbering some kind of nonsense that even I didn't understand. I wasn't making any sense. My brother had recorded my voice during a conversation I'd had with my parents. The conversation was benign. It was my speech he wanted me to hear. "This is how you sound now, Hannah," he said. His eyes bore into me as though he was looking into my soul. "This is how you sound all the time." My mouth dropped open and Cameron shook his head and marched out of my room. To me, his march was more of a statement: *I give up, I'm done waiting for you to get better. It's too painful. I don't want to see you anymore, at least, not this Hannah.*

"Me either," I said to myself after he was gone.

Even after the peace I'd felt in the cornfield, I was still numbing with pills and the airplane-size bottles of alcohol I had hidden around my room. I'd even brought some bottles back from my trip to Kansas, where I'd stocked up at a convenience store next to my hotel. Before Cameron's visit I had fooled myself into believing that, when the time was right, I'd wean myself off the prescription pills and alcohol chasers, but I kept pushing back the right time because it never was right.

Seeing my brother so disillusioned and so

disappointed really shook me. I thought I saw disdain in his eyes. I realized that if I didn't finally face myself and who I had become, I was going to lose my brother's respect and probably my brother. I spent the next day or so debating with myself over what Cameron had said. I loved my brother more than anything in the world, but I was still in so much pain.

I thought about how when I first got home from the hospital I couldn't bear to look at myself in the mirror for fear of what I would see. After a while, Mom arranged my kaboodle of makeup and hair products on the bathroom vanity, I think hoping that I'd be inspired to use them. I've always loved bright lipsticks, and I had a full collection of colors. One day, without thinking, I grabbed tubes of pink-, red-, and maroon-colored lipsticks and began writing on the bathroom mirror. At that point, I still couldn't write with my right hand because it was so badly damaged, so, using my left hand, I scrawled pictures of vines and trees and wrote messages to myself like "Hannah, you are not alone. The universe hears your cries at night," and "Hannah, you will see beauty within your tragedy, so keep your chin up babe." But I still wasn't even close to being there.

The sight of my skin sickened me, and I continued to feel the emptiness of the hole in my heart where my friends had once been. I wasn't sure I was ready to face my pain head-on, not raw. Then I thought: "I have fallen so deep in a pit of snakes, what could be worse than this?" I'd made up my mind. I wanted to get better and I couldn't get there by myself. I needed help. A couple of days passed and I approached my parents one night after dinner. "I can't live like this anymore," I blurted out. "This is not the way I want to live my life. I need help and I want to go away to someplace where I can get the help I need." A moment went by and a palpable wave of relief washed over the room. My secret was out, but it hadn't been a secret at all. My parents said they'd been worried sick about me but they hadn't known how to approach me with their concerns. I asked Papa to find me a place where I could get the help I needed to continue healing my body and my soul.

Within a week, I was on a plane to a holistic healing center in Washington State. I checked my phone and my laptop and all of my other personal possessions at the door and began a four-week recovery program. Mandatory classes were held six hours a day. At first I resented being there, and I fought the counselors on everything from not being allowed to have my phone to the evening curfew. I wrote my parents and complained bitterly about the people and the program. But I stayed.

I began to let my guard down with both the staff and the other patients. During group sessions, I talked about the boys and the guilt I felt over their deaths. People seemed to really grasp the enormity of what I was dealing with, maybe because many of them were being treated for trauma. I tried to give back as much as I was getting. Rather than focus on myself and my loss, I reached out to one girl who had been sexually abused and was suffering from an eating disorder, and another who was chronically depressed and had tried committing suicide on a number of occasions. Helping them helped me. With the aid of natural supplements recommended by the doctors on staff, I began weaning off the myriad of prescription drugs I was taking — for everything from pain to anxiety to sleeplessness to depression. I began to feel hopeful.

I'd been there for about two weeks when, late one afternoon, after my classes were done for the day, I took a walk toward the ocean and found myself exploring a sweet, sultry town along the way. The sun was shining bright and, as I was exploring the pretty shops and galleries, I suddenly realized that both my mind and my body felt healthy and free. I didn't have any physical pain, and for the first time in nine months, my head was clear and my heart felt light. I looked down at my skin and rather than seeing lesions and scars I saw the beauty of being alive. A burst of energy surged through my body and I wanted to shout, "I want to live! I mean really live!" When I told the story at my next group therapy sessions, everyone cheered. After that, every evening I walked to the ocean to sit on the sand and watch the sunset. I was enthralled by the beauty of the exotic colors of the afternoon sun on the landscape. I had never looked at a sunset that way before. It was as if I was seeing it for the very first time. I never wanted those evenings to end, but I knew they had to.

I returned home on Christmas Eve. Charity and Cameron were already there. Everyone was excited to see me. We all attended a candlelight church service then returned home for our Christmas Eve ritual, when we all gathered around Dad while he read the Christmas story and we each got to open a single gift, which usually ended up being three or four.

As we settled into the living room, waiting for Papa to read, I took off my stockings and sat on the floor with my bare legs stretched out before me. I looked around the room at each of my family members. "I want you to touch my skin," I said. My parents and Charity and Cameron knelt around me and put their hands on my burned leg. I began to cry, but my tears weren't sad or bitter, they were tears of gratitude. "I know I've been a basket case for the last few months," I said. "But I just want to let you know that I love all of you so much. You've meant the world to me as I've gone through this and I'm happy to be home with you. I'm getting better and I feel so good. My skin is healing and my mind is clearer than it's ever been. This has been the hardest time of my life and you've all been there for me. I want to tell you that I'm back."

Papa and Mom and Charity huddled close to me. Everyone was crying. "I love you," I said. "We love you, Hannah," they replied. "We love you so much." I felt so blessed to have the family I did.

That was a momentous time for me. I began to forgive myself for the death of my friends and made a commitment to turn my anger over losing them into determination to do something to make them proud of me. For the first time since the crash, happiness seemed almost plausible. After rehab, my skin had taken on a voice of her own, and she had a way with words. When I was feeling overwhelmed and weak, she reminded me of the courage and strength it took to come as far as I had. When I felt shackled by my pain, she reminded me that everyone feels pain, and she encouraged me to see that mine was evidence that my body and my soul were on the mend. Every day I felt her healing me more. Then, one night, in a dream I saw her begin to morph and fade. I cried out, "Please stop! Where are you going? I am just beginning to be able to touch you, to accept you, to love you!" I realized that I had actually become quite fond of my new skin. I woke up, expecting my scars to be gone. When they were still there, radiant and smooth, I sighed with relief.

It was at that moment that I realized that I was free.

# EPILOGUE

I have learned many lessons during my recovery. Lessons about beauty and what matters. Lessons about family and friends and love. Just the other night, while Mom was making homemade vegetable soup, and we waited for Papa to come home for dinner, I sat by the lake behind our house, thinking about how fortunate I am to have parents who took care of me, but also encouraged me to become my own person. It's really quite extraordinary that by showing me unconditional love and support, they gave me the confidence and the gumption to get out there and ask questions and seek my own answers about faith and God.

For months after the crash, I couldn't even hold a book with my burned hands. But recently I grabbed one from my bedroom shelf. It turned out to be a volume of Paulo Coelho's work that a friend had sent me in the hospital, *By the River Piedra, I Sat*

*Down and Wept.* I cracked open the book and the pages fell onto each other before settling on an early page.

I began reading.

"Rarely do we realize that we are in the midst of the extraordinary. Miracles occur all around us. Signs from God show us the way, angels plead to be heard but we pay little attention because we have been taught that we must follow certain formulas and rules if we want to find God. We do not realize that God is anywhere we allow Him/Her to enter."

I closed the book and smiled. In Coelho's words, I realized that all along I had been looking for God in all the wrong places. Or, rather, I hadn't *not* found Him. I hadn't let Him in. I was so busy looking for "proof" that I hadn't been paying attention to what was right in front of my eyes.

So there it was. The answer I had been seeking for most of my life. I had been taught that God could only be perceived in certain prescribed ways, but after the crash, after everything that followed, I now realized that the God I had been searching for was right there all the time. I just needed to allow myself to see the signs, and they were everywhere. In the beauty of nature, and the wonder of love. In the circumstances that converged to spare me an early death. In the courage of my friends in the last minutes of their lives. In the legacy of Austin and Garrett. In the hope I feel for my future.

I have experienced the miracles. I have heard the angels. I have seen God. I see Him everywhere now. In the majesty of beautiful summer nights that I almost didn't get to see. In the sweet deeds of friends and the kindness of strangers. In my mother's gentle reassurances, and the loving eyes of my father as he wraps my hand in his and sits by my bed when I am too afraid to fall asleep, because, sometimes even now when I do, it is May 11, 2012, again and I am back in that plane, looking into the faces of the people I love as we prepare to die.

Everywhere I go now, I carry a remnant of my past in my pocket, a single shard of metal I collected from the crash site when I went back there. Most people would look at it and see just a rusty piece of scrap metal, but it's the most precious thing I own. When I get on an airplane, I hold it close to my heart and hum an old hymn or say a prayer. At night, I place it on the desk, next to my bed, beside the rosary my sister brought me from Spain. To me it's a token of what was and what can be.

Despite what I have been through, mine is a story of hope. And faith. Hope from knowing that, even through great adversity, we can live good and purposeful lives. Faith in knowing that we can see the divine, if only we open our eyes. It is a story of perseverance and finding light in life's darkest moments. Above all, it is a love story about three friends whose bond cannot be broken by death.

Coelho wrote, "To love is to be in communion with the other and to discover in that other the spark of God." I loved Austin and Garrett. They are gone, but their dreams live within me. Because of them, in honor of them, I will find a way to make the world a better place in a way that would make them proud. In them, I have seen the spark of God, and that has given me the courage and the will to go forward.

# AFTERWORD

I was first approached to write a book while I was in the hospital, heavily sedated on narcotics for excruciating pain from my burns. I couldn't imagine what to write about because I wasn't even coherent. But late that night I had a clear flashback to a conversation I'd had with Austin before the crash. He'd told me he had a vision to change the lives of victimized women all over the world. Austin wanted to start an organization called Mirror Tree that would redefine what it meant to be a beautiful woman. No matter your age, race, ethnicity, socioeconomic class, or environmental conditioning, we all deserve a shot at contributing to our world in a meaningful way, and that journey begins from within. From the moment he told me about it, I wanted to help make Austin's vision come true, and we were in cahoots to create Mirror Tree long before the airplane crashed.

Back during my first semester of grad school at Oklahoma State University, I happened upon a cultural studies class that became a favorite of mine. I was young and naïve, just starting out in graduate-level academia. The class explored psychological issues of race and ethnicity, and as part of it, we studied the plight of refugees. I realized that different environmental, political, and socioeconomic factors place layers of challenges on these many innocent lives.

Everything changed for me in the airplane crash where my four friends were killed and I was severely burned. After the accident I realized that what was the most horrific day of my life is everyday living for many refugee women around the world. And for that reason and to honor Austin and his vision, all of the proceeds from this book go directly to Mirror Tree, the nonprofit I'm in the process of forming. My aim is to create hope in a dark world. Female refugees are victims with no one to defend their honor, no one to protect them, and no one to rescue them from unholy crimes. At Mirror Tree we will research and create opportunities for people in the United States to help rehabilitate and reintegrate female refugees and others suffering from the aftereffects of rape, genocide, and loss of identity. Mirror

Tree is committed to doing everything it can to give hope to those victims. By buying and reading this book, you're helping to memorialize Austin and continue the good work that he began, and for that I thank you from the bottom of my heart.

Hannah Luce, August 2013

# ACKNOWLEDGMENTS

Gratitude to Brandi Bowles and Peter McGuigan at Foundry Literary and Media for seeing the beauty and the possibilities of this story and putting us together to write it. Judith Curr at Atria, having your confidence meant everything. Sarah Durand at Atria and Beth Adams at Howard, editors extraordinaire, your insight and talent are matched only by your sensitivity and kindness. Thanks aren't enough. (And welcome to the world, little Lucy!) To Chief Duane Banzet, thank you for being willing to share your memories of that painful day and, even more, for doing God's work with kindness and compassion. Thank you, Heather and Linda for piecing together parts of the story that only you could, but most of all for your humanity in a time of crisis.

Finally, to the families and loved ones of Austin Anderson, Garrett Coble, Luke Sheets, and Stephen Luth, the goal here was to honor your beloved young men by showing them for the brave, faithful, extraordinary people they were. Austin loved to quote from the movie *Braveheart* — "Every man dies, not every man really *lives.*" They really lived. May the brightness of their souls help to light the way for us all.

The employees of Thorndike Press hope you have enjoyed this Large Print book. All our Thorndike, Wheeler, and Kennebec Large Print titles are designed for easy reading, and all our books are made to last. Other Thorndike Press Large Print books are available at your library, through selected bookstores, or directly from us.

For information about titles, please call:
  (800) 223-1244

or visit our Web site at:
  http://gale.cengage.com/thorndike

To share your comments, please write:
  Publisher
  Thorndike Press
  10 Water St., Suite 310
  Waterville, ME 04901